Tales from the Yankee Dugout

Quips, Quotes & Anecdotes about the Bronx Bombers

by
Ken McMillan

Illustrations
by Bob Jackson

Sports Publishing Inc.
www.SportsPublishingInc.com

Director of Production: Susan M. McKinney
Book design, project manager: Jennifer L. Polson
Cover design: Julie L. Denzer

Front cover photo by Dan Farrell, *Daily News*.
Back cover photo by Dan Cronin, *Daily News*.

ISBN: 1-58261-054-1
Library of Congress Number: 00-101396

Printed in the United States.

Sports Publishing Inc.
804 North Neil
Champaign, IL 61820
www.SportsPublishingInc.com

*This book is dedicated to my mother, Rita,
and late father, Wallace.*

✿

I hope I've made you proud.

ACKNOWLEDGMENTS

Most writers dream of writing books, but very few actually develop an idea and follow it through to its conclusion. In this case, the idea of compiling short stories on the New York Yankees came from The Dreaming Dog Group. I thank the agency for the opportunity to take the idea and run with it. Without The Dog's assistance and faith in a rookie author, this book would not be in your hands. I would also like to thank Mike Pearson of Sports Publishing Inc. for agreeing to publish this book.

I must thank the librarian of my research, faithful Yankees fan Craig Anderson, for supplying me with a seemingly endless supply of resource material on the Yankees.

Valuable technical assistance was provided by Gary Carter and Jeff Ehmann. Without their input my words would have remained locked forever within outdated word processing programs. Their advice and hands-on help moved the project forward at a critical juncture.

Finally, I must thank my many friends and family members who saw to it I kept this project moving in a positive direction. Special thanks goes out to Gary Carter, Diana Kazolias and my mother, Rita McMillan, for their caring and understanding through a painstaking process.

CONTENTS

Yogi Berra 1
Jim Bouton 9
Bronx Battlers 15
Al DeVormer 17
Bill Dickey 18
Joe DiMaggio 20
Fightin' Words 27
Whitey Ford 35
Oscar Gamble 41
Lou Gehrig 45
Jake Gibbs 51
Lefty Gomez 53
Goose Gossage 56
Ron Guidry 58
Steve Hamilton 60
Tommy Henrich 61
Miller Huggins 63
Reggie Jackson 65
Derek Jeter 68
Steve Kemp 72
Don Larsen 74
Phil Linz 77
Don Lock 79
Sparky Lyle 80
Mickey Mantle 85
Roger Maris 92
Billy Martin 97
Don Mattingly 104
Joe McCarthy 111

Wilcy Moore 115
Thurman Munson 117
Graig Nettles 123
Gabe Paul 128
Joe Pepitone 130
Gaylord Perry 134
Fritz Peterson 136
Lou Piniella 137
Willie Randolph 144
Allie Reynolds 145
Mickey Rivers 147
Phil Rizzuto 150
Charles "Red" Ruffing 155
Babe Ruth 156
Rollie Sheldon 174
George Steinbrenner 175
Casey Stengel 179
Joe Torre 185
David Wells 188
Dave Winfield 191
Butch Wyneger 195
Yankee Miscellaneous 196
Yankee Stadium 201
Don Zimmer 205
Bibliography 207

Yogi Berra

Listen To These!

Yogi Berra's fame was born out of 14 World Series appearances with the Yankees (which included 10 titles) and 15 consecutive All-Star Games.

His legend grew with his familiar malapropisms, known as "Yogi-isms." A sampling:

- "It ain't over till it's over."
- "It's deja vu all over again."
- Speaking of two nights held in his honor in New York and his hometown of St. Louis: "I want to thank all of the people for making this night possible."
- Asked what time it was, he said, "You mean now?"
- "A nickel ain't worth a dime anymore."
- "Baseball is 90 percent mental. The other half is physical."

- "If the people don't want to come out to the ballpark, nobody's going to stop them."
- During spring training a trainer asked Berra what hat size he required. His reply: "I don't know. I'm not in shape yet."
- Speaking of a restaurant, he said, "Nobody goes there anymore. It's too crowded."
- "I usually take a two-hour nap, from one to four."
- "I'd rather be the Yankees catcher than the president, and that makes me pretty lucky, I guess, because I could never be the president."
- "I've been with the Yankees for 17 years watching games and learning. You can see a lot by observing."
- Mary Lindsay, the wife of New York City major John Lindsay, once commented how Berra appeared nice and cool one day, to which Berra replied, "You don't look so hot yourself."
- Johnny Bench received a telegram from Berra after the Cincinnati Reds star broke the Yankee's all-time home run record for catchers. It read: "Congratulations on breaking my record. I always thought it would stand until it was broken."
- "If you come to a fork in the road, take it."

Outfielder Charley Keller spoke fondly of Berra and his Yogi-isms. "He had a way of saying things that made you think and smile and then say, 'I would never say it that way, but I know what he means.' Sometimes it seemed to make more sense the way he said it than the regular way, and that may have been a part of his charm."

Quote, End Quote

❝ What you have to do when you consider Yogi is think about where he started and where he ended. I don't mean that he was poor—a lot of us were that. I mean that all he ever wanted to be was a baseball player, and almost everyone told him he couldn't be one. He not only became a ballplayer, he became a great one and one of the most loved and respected of the last 50 years. Every time I see him I feel good."

— Former teammate Jerry Coleman

You Need To Know This

How did Lawrence Peter Berra earn the nickname "Yogi?"

His friends had seen a Hindu fakir in a movie sitting still with arms and legs folded. It reminded them of Berra as he sat between innings.

The Master Motivator

Yogi Berra had a very competitive drive as a player, and he would try any method to get one of his pitchers to perform better.

With Vic Raschi, Berra used to insult him, calling him "Onion Head," or challenging his performance.

"Is that as hard as you can throw it?" Berra would ask Raschi if a fastball didn't live up to the catcher's expectations.

Berra was also a chatterbox behind the plate, trying to find a mental edge by getting into a player's head as he stood in the batter's box.

Sometimes it was more than words that came out of Berra's mouth.

"I knew that when the hitter said, 'Yogi, shut up,' I was going good," Berra said.

Ken "Hawk" Harrelson recalls his rookie season with Kansas City and how his game with the Yankees was being televised by NBC. Down 0-2 in the count, Harrelson was still thinking about his mom watching on television back in Georgia when he felt something warm on the back of his sock. By time he realized what had happened, Whitey Ford blew strike three past him.

"Yogi had spit on my calf just before Whitey delivered," Harrelson said. "I was dumbfounded. As I turned, my mouth hanging open, I am sure, Yogi said, 'Welcome to the big leagues, kid.'"

A Thriller

" In some ways wearing a Yankee uniform for 25 years was the biggest thrill I ever had . . . . Putting on the pinstripes was the best thing that ever happened to me . . . . Being a Yankee was all it was cracked up to be and then some."

— Yogi Berra

Discipline

Known as a free swinger at the plate, manager Bucky Harris wanted Berra to show more patience. So Berra—who was once told by Boston Red Sox great hitter Ted Williams that he was "an awful sight" at the plate and gave hitting "a bad name"—went up to the plate and took three pitches for strikes.

When Harris demanded to know what he was doing up there, Berra shot back, "It's your fault. How do you expect a guy to hit and think, to think and hit at the same time?"

Of course, Williams also heaped great praise on Berra's ability to hit in the clutch.

"He looked like hell, but what happened when he attacked the ball was right out of a computer. He could move the runner, and move him late in the game like no one else I ever saw play the game."

He's No House Boy

Bobby Richardson was asked to stay with Berra and his wife in his New Jersey home.

Pulling up to the expansive manse, Richardson asked Berra how many rooms there were.

Said Yogi: "I don't know. Carmen takes care of that."

Temperature Check

Trainer Dennis Liborio was watching Berra gingerly step into a whirlpool and then watching the catcher sort of jump up and down without saying anything.

He asked Berra if the water was too hot.

"How hot is it supposed to be?" Berra asked.

Gracious Close

" Baseball is a great way to spend your life if you are successful, and I was. Going to a game with your family is also a great thing to do. It can make you understand your kids, and they can get to know you. All those good things. It is a wonderful thing for you to do in the afternoon, at night, and from April until October. All summer. You can start when the first robin builds a nest and see baseball until the geese fly south."

— Yogi Berra on baseball

Jim Bouton

Accentuate The Positive

Managers sometimes have to coax their players through their troubles, whether they be physical or emotional.

The power of positive persuasion is something Johnny Keane used to his advantage.

Mickey Mantle recalled a conversation that went as follows:

"How do your legs feel today, Mick?"

"Not too good," Mantle replied.

"Yes, but how do they feel?"

"It hurts when I run, the right one especially. I can't stride on it or anything."

"Well, do you think you can play?" Keane would ask.

"I don't know. I guess I can play. Yeah, hell, what the hell. Sure I can play," Mantle said, giving in.

"Good. Great. We need you out there. Unless you're hurt—unless it really hurts you. I don't want you to play if you're hurt."

"No, it's okay. I hurt, but it's okay. I'll watch it."

"Good, good. We sure need you."

Mantle's teammates would get a kick out of this. Jim Bouton would play the role of Keane when he'd ask Mantle, "Mick, how does your leg feel?"

"Well, it's severed at the knee," Mantle would deadpan.

"Yes, but does it hurt?"

"No, I scotch-taped it back into place."

"And how's your back?"

"My back is broken in seven places."

"Can you swing the bat?"

"Yeah, I can swing. If I can find some more scotch tape."

"Great. Well, get in there then. We need you."

S truggling pitchers will listen to just about anyone to cure their ills.

Jim Bouton was in such a sorry state he actually listened to some tips offered by restaurant owner Toots Shor.

"Once when I was going bad," Bouton said, "he told me my whole problem was that I was striding three inches too far and if I just shortened up on the stride by those three inches everything would be fine. I was so desperate I actually tried it." He added, "It didn't help."

Just How Close?

How close was Jim Bouton to becoming a one-game major leaguer?

Inches.

In his first Yankee Stadium start as a rookie in 1962, Bouton opened with eight pitches out of the strike zone. With the count at 3-1 on the third Washington Senators hitter, Bouton threw another ball. Or so he thought, as did manager Ralph Houk, who was stepping out of the dugout. Turns out, the home plate umpire called a strike. Bouton survived not only the first inning but the entire game.

He shut out the Senators on seven hits and seven walks. Left fielder Hector Lopez bailed Bouton out with four leaping catches.

Following the game, Bouton walked back into the locker room just in time to see Mickey Mantle laying down the final white towel, completing a carpet to the victor's locker.

"I'll never forget him for that," Bouton said.

Ol' No. 56, And Don't Forget It!

J im Bouton was handed uniform number 56 during spring training in 1962. When it appeared he was going to make the team, clubhouse manager Pete Sheehy said he could give Bouton number 27 to wear.

"I told him I'd keep 56 because I wanted it to remind me of how close I was to not making the club."

The Doc

E ver hear this Henny Youngman joke?

Guy goes into a doctor's office, sticks his arm out and says, "Doctor, doctor. It hurts when I do this."

"Well, don't do that," the doctor replied.

That's the way some Yankees felt about visiting Dr. Sidney Gaynor.

Jim Bouton broke the thumb on his pitching hand while toiling in the minors in Auburn, New York. The good doc removed the cast from Bouton's hand, examined it closely and told him he had a broken thumb and that he shouldn't bump it into anything.

A couple years later, Bouton went for another checkup. Gaynor put Bouton through some stretching exercises and then told him, "You got a sore arm."

"Yeah, I know. It hurts when I throw."

Gaynor scowled at Bouton and offered, "If it's sore, don't throw."

"How long?" Bouton inquired. "I don't know," Gaynor said. "When it starts feeling better then you can start throwing again."

Bronx Battlers

F ive Yankees were waiting for some last-minute woman chasing before a midnight curfew one night in St. Louis, where Billy Martin caught the ears of five women coming out of the lobby of the Chase Hotel.

However, five male friends also came out and were upset with the players' advances. A fight was about to ensue when Ralph Houk and Hank Bauer started to argue over who was going to start the brawl. It was decided Houk would, since any injury to him wouldn't hurt the club as much.

Houk proved to be a tough fighter. He knocked down one of the men three times, with a distraught Mickey Mantle going over each time to pick the man up and wipe blood from his face with a handkerchief.

Finally, the beaten man grabbed Mantle's arm and said, "Buddy, I don't know who the hell you are, but would you mind staying out of this fight?"

R alph Houk was also at the center of a bar brawl, also in St. Louis, that nearly turned ugly.

A female bartender took exception to comments made by one of the Yankee ballplayers, and soon a handful of bar bouncers showed up. One of them pulled a gun, and Houk reacted by breaking a bottle and holding the jagged edge to the man's throat. All together, the Yankee players backed out of the bar and hopped a cab out of trouble.

Al DeVormer

B ackup catcher Al DeVormer spent an undistin-
guished 46-game career with the Yankees in 1921
and 1922. Most notable about the Michigan native—
besides his occasional agitation in the clubhouse—was
his penchant for doing crazy things.

On one occasion, DeVormer jumped into Lake
Michigan in his street clothes just to win a $25 bet.

Bill Dickey

Best Catcher?

B ill Dickey is often referred to as the best Yankee
catcher of all time, impressive considering his heady
company.

He hit better than .300 for 11 seasons.

Wrote Dan Daniel: "Dickey isn't just a catcher.
He's a ballclub. He isn't just a player. He's an influence."

In Control

D ickey was a tough ballplayer behind the dish. On July 4, 1932, a collision took place between Dickey and Carl Reynolds of Washington. Words were exchanged and Dickey broke Reynolds' jaw with a single punch.

Dickey was fined $1,000 and sat out a month.

Joe DiMaggio

The Streak

Baseball historians have argued over what baseball record will go down next. Mark McGwire and Sammy Sosa played their part in eclipsing Roger Maris' 61-homer record during a glorious 1998 season.

Near the end of the 1998 season, Baltimore Orioles infielder Cal Ripken Jr. put a coda on the consecutive games streak that he had lifted from the Iron Horse, Yankee great Lou Gehrig.

That leaves Joe DiMaggio's 56-game consecutive hitting streak in 1941 near the top of everyone's list.

"The streak," as it became known, started quietly on May 15 and culminated with a record crowd on July 17. DiMaggio's feats lifted a nation, which was poised on the brink of world war. His batting average

stood at .306 when DiMaggio stepped up to face Chicago White Sox left-hander Edgar Smith.

DiMaggio singled in the first inning, a simple act which opened a drama that would catch the attention of a nation. In fact, the streak wasn't noticed for weeks.

A month into the streak, DiMaggio's legendary status grew, as did his popularity. He was swarmed by well-wishers as he attended the Joe Louis-Billy Conn heavyweight title fight.

"There were so many people asking for his autograph that he had almost as many cops around him as the fighters," friend George Solotaire said.

While some pitchers took to pitching away from DiMaggio—not a bad idea considering his average was in the .350 range—others did not fear him, and usually paid for it.

St. Louis Browns rookie Bob Muncrief served up an eighth-inning single to stretch the streak to 36. Browns manager Luke Sewell demanded to know why he decided to pitch to DiMaggio. Said Muncrief: "I wasn't going to walk him. That wouldn't have been fair—to him or to me. Hell, he's the greatest player I ever saw."

Even when pitchers threw away from DiMaggio, sometimes luck and a little skill were on his side. Johnny Babich of the Philadelphia A's was ready to serve up a walk when DiMaggio reached for an outside pitch and lined a shot through Babich's legs. Noted DiMaggio: "(Manager Joe) McCarthy was great to me during the streak. He let me hit the 3-0 pitch quite a few times."

Even DiMaggio's teammates came to his aid. With the streak on the line against the Browns, McCarthy granted Tommy Henrich's request for an eighth-inning bunt to avoid a potential double-play ball that likely would have put an end to DiMaggio's streak. Henrich sacrificed and DiMaggio then doubled on the first delivery from Eldon Auker.

In Washington, D.C., a fan stole DiMaggio's bat, the one he had just used to tie George Sisler's American League record streak of 41. DiMaggio was upset because he had taken some precious weight off the 36-inch, 36-ounce piece of wood with sandpaper. Fortunately, friends of DiMaggio later recovered the bat from the Newark, New Jersey, fan who had lifted it and then made the mistake of bragging about it.

The streak came to an end on July 17 at Cleveland Stadium. A taxi driver had taken DiMaggio and pitcher Lefty Gomez to the ballpark. His words to DiMaggio proved prophetic. "I got a feeling that if you don't get a hit the first time up, they're gonna stop you tonight," the driver said, raising Gomez's dander a bit. "What the hell is this?" he demanded. "What are you trying to do—jinx him?"

Indians third baseman Ken Keltner robbed DiMaggio of hits in the first and seventh innings. In the eighth, reliever Jim Bagby Jr. came on to face DiMaggio. He hit a shot that shortstop Lou Boudreau fielded off a bad hop to start a double play.

New York Sun writer Herb Goren wrote the next day: "DiMaggio rounded first base, picked up his glove and trotted to center field. There was no kicking of dirt, no shaking of the head."

The Other Streak

The 56-game streak was not DiMaggio's longest. He hit in 61 consecutive games with the San Francisco Seals of the Pacific Coast League in 1933.

Threaded

Image was always important for Joe DiMaggio, and he dressed the part wearing fine suits. In 1936, he was voted one of the 10 best-dressed men in America.

And Now, The Lyrics

In the midst of the 56-game hitting streak, a disc jockey named Alan Courtney penned lyrics to honor Joe DiMaggio. His copyrighted tune "Jolting Joe DiMaggio" goes like this:

Who started baseball's famous streak
That's got us all aglow?
He's just a man and not a freak.
Jolting Joe DiMaggio.
Joe . . . Joe . . . DiMaggio . . .
we want you on our side.
From Coast to Coast, that's all you hear
Of Joe the One-Man Show.
He's glorified the horsehide sphere,
Jolting Joe DiMaggio.
Joe . . . Joe . . . DiMaggio . . .
we want you on our side.
He'll live in baseball's Hall of Fame.
He got there blow-by-blow
Our kids will tell their kids his name.
Jolting Joe DiMaggio.

Big City? Hah!

J oe DiMaggio retired at the age of 36.

In an address to fans on Joe DiMaggio Day in 1949, he spoke of being made welcome. "When I was in San Francisco, Lefty O'Doul told me: 'Joe, don't let the big city scare you. New York is the friendliest town in the world.' This day proves it. I want to thank my fans, my friends, my manager, Casey Stengel; my teammates, the gamest, fightingest bunch of guys that ever lived. And I want to thank the good Lord for making me a Yankee."

On The Big Screen

J oe DiMaggio made his Hollywood debut in 1937 in a movie called "Manhattan Merry-Go Round." He also appeared in the 1951 film "Angels in the Outfield."

Fightin' Words

Gonna Fly Now

Not all the fighting was left to the players. Following Game 5 of the 1981 World Series, owner George Steinbrenner got involved with two fans in a hotel elevator.

"I clocked them," Steinbrenner said proudly, even with his hand bandaged.

"There are two guys in this town looking for their teeth."

On the flight back to New York the next day, Lou Piniella passed by Steinbrenner and asked, "How are you doing, Rocky?"

That prompted a huge grin from the owner.

Catchers In The Fray

The Yankees' pennant drive of 1974 was waylaid by a brawl between catchers Bill Sudakis and Rick Dempsey.

Neither backstop was seeing much action behind Thurman Munson. Sudakis decided he would razz Dempsey about it as the Yankee bus made its way to a Milwaukee hotel.

Once there, Dempsey and Sudakis tried to go through the hotel's revolving door at the same time and the door jammed. Once freed, Dempsey threw a punch at Sudakis. Sudakis lunged at Dempsey and the pair rolled over a table and onto a couch.

Bobby Murcer jumped into the fray to play peacemaker, and ended up hurting his hand. He was put out of the lineup and the Yanks lost the pennant by a game.

Still Old Foes

Sometimes old foes become new teammates, but remain foes.

Case in point: Cliff Johnson and Goose Gossage. Early in the 1979 season, Johnson was steamed about being left out of the lineup one day. Johnson was asked how he had fared against the fire-balling Gossage in previous seasons, but before he could answer, Goose said, "He couldn't hit what he couldn't see," and laughed his way into the clubhouse sauna.

When the pitcher came out again, Johnson confronted Gossage and a huge rolling fight took place. The result was Gossage hurting his right thumb and missing action for the next three months.

Fam-uh-lee?

The Pittsburgh Pirates rode the theme, "We are Family," on the way to their 1979 World Series championship. Two years later, Yankee teammates were at each other's throats before the first pitch of the Fall Classic was thrown out.

The Yankees swept the Oakland A's—managed that strike year by none other than Billy Martin—and decided to celebrate their American League pennant at a Bay area restaurant. As the story goes, Graig Nettles' wife, Ginger, left her purse on her chair as she went to get something to eat. When she got back, the purse was missing and one of Reggie Jackson's guests was sitting in the chair.

An argument ensued, and Graig knocked Reggie down with two punches.

Put Up Your Dukes, Let's Get Down To It!

There's no Yankee fighting legend as good as Battling Billy Martin.

He fought with teammates, opponents, his own players, bar patrons and a marshmallow salesman.

Phil Rizzuto was quoted as saying, "Billy is like a gunfighter in those westerns. There is always some young guy who wants to take him on and prove something and Billy can't back away."

A 1985 trip to Baltimore produced back-to-back brawls for Billy. On the first night, an angry bridegroom accused Martin of insulting his newlywed wife, an argument ensued and the pair had to be separated by Yankee players and bartenders.

The next evening, disgruntled pitcher Ed Whitson and Martin went at it after the manager decided not to use Whitson for a start. What started as an argument between Whitson and another bar patron turned into an all-out punching and kicking brawl between Martin and Whitson. The pitcher ended up breaking Martin's right arm with a kick. Incredibly, neither Whitson nor Martin received any punishment from Steinbrenner.

At season's end, Martin demanded a raise of salary to $500,000, or he might not return. Not amused, Steinbrenner hit the right chord when he surmised, "Well, let's see. That'll be $200,000 for managing the team and $300,000 for being the first challenger to (heavyweight boxing champion) Michael Spinks."

Pitching A Fit

Sometimes a fight isn't actually a fight. In a May 1969 game between the Washington Senators and New York Yankees, Bobby Murcer homered off Senator Marty Pattin.

The next time up Pattin sailed a pitch over Murcer's head. Murcer eventually reached base and came in high with his spikes on a slide into Ray Oyler, prompting a bench-clearing brawl.

While Murcer and Oyler apologized to one another while at the bottom of the pile, ex-Yankee Jim Bouton decided to pair up on the outside of the fray with Fritz Peterson. The old friends decided to put on a little show.

"How's your wife?" Bouton asked. "Give me a fake punch to the ribs."

"She's fine," Peterson replied. "You can punch me in the stomach. Not too hard."

Eventually, Peterson forced Bouton to the ground and the pair rolled around for effect, prompting two umpires to rush over to tell them to knock it off.

"But we're only kidding," Bouton said. "We're old roommates."

The umpire told them to break it up anyway.

Stupid Ballplayer Tricks

The heat of battle will force players to do many stupid things.

On July 26, 1922, first baseman Wally Pipp misplayed a ball at first base, just another defensive lapse that outfielder Babe Ruth had been riding Pipp about for weeks.

Pipp was convinced Ruth would say something at the close of the inning, and sure enough Ruth did.

"For God's sake, Pipp," Ruth said, only to be hit in the face several times by the quick-swinging Pipp.

Having been pulled apart, Ruth told Pipp this incident would be settled after the game.

As it turns out, 15 runs would be scored in the final three innings. The Yankees beat the St. Louis Browns, 11-6, with the help of two home runs by Ruth.

Following the game a joyous Ruth bounded into the clubhouse only to be met by Pipp.

"I'm ready," Pipp said.

Ruth had forgotten his vow made in haste earlier and then waved Pipp away.

"Oh, Christ, forget it."

Howdy, Y'all

Not all of Ruth's fights took place at the ballpark. The Yankees conducted spring training in 1921 at Shreveport, Louisiana.

Sometimes, Ruth and some teammates headed into the countryside to find a roadhouse bar. One night the partying got too loud and a local man took exception.

An argument ensued, but peace was restored. The agitator left in a huff, as did Ruth later on in the Essex the city had given him for use during camp.

Pitcher Harry Harper noticed that a car left right after Ruth's did and he suspected there would be trouble.

Harper and some teammates got into Harper's car and drove off to follow. They found Ruth's car on the side of the road and Ruth holding his hands up while the same man from the bar was pointing a gun at him.

Harper drove his car right at the man, who jumped to the side and was grabbed by Ruth.

Harper, who later would become the sheriff of Bergen County, New Jersey, disarmed the man and sent him away.

C atcher Bill Dickey once was suspended 30 games for breaking a Washington player's jaw.

He did it with one punch during a dispute at home plate.

Whitey Ford

Oh, Waiter . . .

When Whitey Ford and Mickey Mantle got together, their teammates had to prep for any practical joke.

When Joe Pepitone and Phil Linz made the club,
Ford and Mantle told the new guys to get dressed up
and meet them at a Detroit restaurant called The Flame.

Ford and Mantle were going to pick up the tab.
All they had to do was ask for Mantle's favorite table.

Pepitone and Linz were so excited about being
invited to dinner with the team leaders they told everyone about it.

A half-hour cab ride was the capper to the cruelest
joke.

The establishment was in the middle of an urban slum. A sign over the door read: THE FLAME. No Mantle. No Ford. No table.

The Craftsmen

Whitey Ford won 236 games in 16 seasons with the Yankees, with 10 more coming in World Series play. The crafty left-hander used every trick in his arsenal to baffle hitters.

The mud ball, or "mudder" as it was known, was positively vicious as it sailed in or out, up or down on hitters.

Catcher Ellie Howard was Ford's accomplice, often loading the ball up with mud before throwing it back to the mound. He'd cover it up by pretending to lose his balance and righting himself with his hand while the ball was in it.

Ford also liked to use his wedding ring. By gouging slices into the ball, a pitch could dive down, sail up or take a little hop before reaching the plate. When that trick was discovered, Howard would use the buckle on his shin guards to nick the ball.

How Do You Spell Relief?

When Ford was pitching on the hill, there was little need to go to the relief staff. To keep his bullpen pals happy, Ford would set up a table in the bullpen, cover it with a checkered tablecloth and place a candle on it. He would then treat his fellow hurlers to some hero sandwiches.

Hit? Where?

Whitey Ford used his sharp wit on his teammates. In 1965, Leon James "Duke" Carmel was a phenom waiting to bust loose, except his bat wouldn't support the claims of Yankee scouts.

Carmel struggled during spring training games in Fort Lauderdale, Florida, prompting Ford to say, "Well, Duke, it looks like you can't hit in southern Florida."

A trip to Tampa didn't help. "Well, Duke, it looks like you're just not a Florida hitter," Ford said.

A few more exhibition games in the South didn't yield hits, either. "Well, Duke, it looks like you just can't hit south of the Mason-Dixon Line."

A 0-for-8 effort in six regular-season games was all the Yankees needed to see to release Carmel.

Golden Arm

October. World Series. Yankee great Whitey Ford on the hill.

It was commonplace.

"You kind of took it for granted around the Yankees that there was always going to be baseball in October," Ford said.

His Yankee teams won 11 American League pennants, allowing Ford the opportunity to start a record 22 World Series games.

Money Ahead

In his retirement speech, Ford said, "I came here in 1950 and I was wearing $50 suits. And I'm leaving wearing $200 suits. And I'm gettin' 'em for $80. So I guess I'm doing all right."

One Wasn't Enough

M ost players earn one nickname during their career. Edward Charles Ford had three: Whitey, Slick and Chairman of the Board.

The Winningest

F ord racked up the most wins in Yankee history, so he always had a warm spot for pitchers of the Senior Circuit. After pitching the clincher of the 1950 World Series against the Phillies, Ford ran into broadcaster Dizzy Dean, formerly of the St. Louis Cardinals. "No wonder you won 30 games," Ford told him. "You were pitching in that crummy National League. I would win 40 in that league myself."

Oscar Gamble

About That House . . .

After being reacquired by the Yankees, Oscar Gamble spent much of the 1983 season living in a hotel.

All the while he had his sights set on a house owned by disgruntled teammate Jerry Mumphrey. Often he'd playfully feed Mumphrey's frustrations in hopes Mumphrey would demand a trade.

"How much longer are you going to live in that hotel?" someone asked Gamble.

"Right up until the time Mumphrey gets traded."

Humor At The End Of The Bench

G amble never was satisfied with the playing time he received, but he always maintained his quick wit.

Told he was batting fifth in one game, Gamble said, "I guess that's better than hitting 12th, where I have been playing."

While razzing Lou Piniella, Gamble said, "When you come up, the left fielder takes a cigarette break. You can't pull the ball anymore. They're going to pull the old Satchel Paige routine on you. Pull all the out-fielders in and sit them around the mound."

Quick! Draw!

F or a while, Gamble was known as "Jesse" to some players.

During contract negotiations with the San Diego Padres one season, Gamble was ready to ask for $1.5 million. Owner Ray Kroc stepped in and gave Gamble a contract ultimatum—Gamble would make $3 million but he had to sign the deal within 10 minutes.

Frankly, he couldn't get the pen out of his pocket fast enough.

Thus, the nickname "Jesse James."

Tie One On

Second baseman Willie Randolph was placed on the disabled list one time leaving Gamble distraught.

It had nothing to do with Randolph's playing ability.

Gamble always had Randolph tie his ties when the team went out on road trips.

He'd get his just due later on, always trying to stir Randolph up with what the newspapers were saying about him.

If nothing was written, Gamble would make things up just to get a reaction.

What I Meant Was . . .

Casey Stengel wasn't the only Yankee who could mangle words and names. Gamble always called reliever Ray Fontenot (FON-ten-no) "Footnote."

When trying to refer to famed actor Efram Zimbalist Jr., Gamble called him "Epplin Zepplin Junior."

Lou Gehrig

Young Lou

L ou Gehrig and Babe Ruth formed the most powerful pair of home run hitters in Major League history. Their Yankee paths would not cross until Gehrig
arrived in 1923, but the two would be linked by reputation years earlier.

Gehrig led Commerce High School to the New
York City scholastic championship during his senior
year. As a result, the newly created *New York Daily News*
sent the Commerce team out west to face Chicago city
champion Lane Tech High School.

Commerce prevailed, 12-6, with Gehrig smashing a grand slam out of the park. Suddenly, Gehrig was
tabbed, "The Babe Ruth of the High Schools."

It was a distinction Gehrig also earned while playing collegiately for Columbia University. He hit seven home runs one season.

He Kept On Ticking

L ou Gehrig was nicknamed The Iron Horse for his incredible consecutive games playing streak of 2,130 games.

Legend has the streak starting with manager Miller Huggins patting Gehrig on the back and telling him to replace Wally Pipp at first base, this taking place on June 1, 1925.

Actually, the day was correct but the first game of Gehrig's streak was a pinch-hitting appearance for rookie Pee Wee Wanninger.

The next day, Gehrig took over the first base duties from Pipp, who had suffered a bad beaning and was being phased out of the lineup.

It must also be noted that Gehrig was drilled in the forehead with a double-play throw in that same game, knocking him senseless. Asked if he wanted to be removed from the contest, Gehrig replied: " Hell, no! It's taken me three years to get into this game. It's going to take more than a crack on the head to get me out."

Fourteen years later, it was the debilitating effects of amyotrophic lateral sclerosis that forced Gehrig out of the lineup.

A side note: Wanninger actually bridged the gap between the record holders for consecutive games. A month earlier Wanninger had replaced Everett Scott, who owned the mark at 1,307 games.

Hey, That's My Job!

Wally Pipp's first brush with Gehrig took place in 1923.

Gehrig had just signed a pro contract with the Yankees—thus concluding an abbreviated college career with Columbia University—when Pipp was enlisted by a National League team to negotiate a contract with Gehrig.

Little did Pipp know at that time that Gehrig was already signed and would have Pipp's job inside of two years.

He Just Knew It

Hall of Famer Ty Cobb recognized Gehrig's greatness from the moment he donned the Yankee uniform.

"Lou Gehrig was the hustlinest ball player I ever saw, and I admired him for it," Cobb said in his Georgia accent.

"When I first saw him break in the lineup, as a rookie, I went and told him just that."

Plenty Tough

How tough was Lou Gehrig?

Consider, in his triple crown championship year of 1934, he fractured a toe and played on.

He also was knocked unconscious by a pitched ball, suffered a severe concussion and was still back in the lineup the next day.

X-rays showed he had broken every finger on both hands at some time in his career, 17 fractures in all—this, on top of all the other assorted injuries.

(Sort Of) Funny Stuff

L ou Gehrig and his wife, Eleanor, were very playful with one another.

They enjoyed roughhousing with one another. They'd wrestle and sometimes box.

One day Eleanor knocked Lou out with a single punch. After he shook off the blur, he burst out in laughter.

Lou's Little Helper?

L ou Gehrig did not abstain from alcohol altogether, but he rarely drank.

However, manager Miller Huggins noticed Gehrig was in the midst of a prolonged batting slump and decided to give his slugger $10 to go out on a bender.

Jake Gibbs

Get The Point?

Talk about the cure being worse than the ailment!
Catcher Jake Gibbs got hit in the hand during
spring training, and a trainer determined a hole had to
be drilled through his fingernail to relieve the pressure.

The drill bit smoked as it bore through Gibbs' nail,
but when it broke through Gibbs recoiled in pain.

The drill remained in the hole as he jumped around
in agony.

You Know What I Mean!

Menu reading was not a strength of Gibbs. He ordered pie a la mode one time and then asked the waitress to put ice cream on it.

Lefty Gomez

Hey, Batter!

What was the secret to Lefty Gomez' pitching success?

"I talk 'em out of hits," Gomez said of the hitters.

Tension-breaker

Trips to the mound produced some of Gomez' best lines.

Catcher Bill Dickey visited one day and asked what they should throw Jimmie Foxx.

Said Gomez: "I don't want to throw him nothin'. Maybe he'll get tired of waitin' and leave." After loading the bases, manager Joe McCarthy took a visit and made the mistake of pointing out that very fact.

"I know they're loaded up," Gomez said. "Do you think I thought they gave me another infield?"

(Un)Desired Result

Talk about lanky—Gomez stood 6-foot-2 and weighed just 150 pounds.

General manager Ed Barrow suggested Gomez put on 20 pounds and then he'd make people forget about 41-game winner Jack Chesbro.

"I put on 20 pounds and almost made them forget Gomez," Gomez later quipped.

Dragging

As injuries and arm problems began to take their toll on the left-hander, Gomez said this of his fastball: "I'm throwing as hard as I ever did but the ball is just not getting there as fast."

Taking Credit

Gomez takes credit for making Joe DiMaggio the great outfielder that he was.

"I made him famous. They didn't know he could go back on a ball until he played behind me," Gomez joked.

Goose Gossage

Waiter, There's A Spy In The Booth

Major League Baseball has often used law enforcement agencies to get the message out to players about the ills of carousing, drugs and gambling.

One year baseball commissioner Bowie Kuhn made it known he had spies out in the bars and restaurants that players frequented.

One day, buddies Rich "Goose" Gossage and Graig Nettles decided they would try to find the spies and, in doing so, frequented a number of bars and eateries in the Milwaukee area. Their conclusion: Kuhn hired mooses.

They had seen one mounted in one bar and then another four hours later.

"That's the second moose we've seen today," Gossage said, figuring he found the spy.

This Way?

It's obvious wildlife and Gossage didn't mix well. Gossage took his wife out to dinner in Boston.

He cracked open the claw of a lobster, and one of the thorns on it went right into the fingernail of his index finger on his pitching hand.

Nettles used the opportunity to needle the pitcher the next day.

"Goose, cheeseburgers don't bite back! What are you trying to do?"

Gossage assured Nettles he was going back to the burgers.

Ron Guidry

Ron Guidry proved to be the catalyst in the Yankees' 1978 championship run, but he almost never made it out of spring training in 1977.

Guidry was getting hit hard, prompting owner George Steinbrenner to go nuts.

Said the Boss to manager Billy Martin: "I got to get rid of him, he can't pitch, I got to get rid of that skinny kid. I'm telling you right now he can't pitch."

Fortunately, Martin and general manager Gabe Paul prevented Steinbrenner from pulling the trigger on a trade.

A year later, Guidry posted a 25-3 record and 1.74 earned run average, helped the Yankees to the American League East Division playoff victory at Boston's Fenway Park and won his lone start in the World Series triumph over the Los Angeles Dodgers.

Steve Hamilton

P'tooey

Chewing tobacco has been a tradition—albeit a bad one—with baseball players for decades.

Pitcher Steve Hamilton not only chewed at the ballpark, he chewed everywhere. Even his living room had a spittoon in the middle of it.

One night while pitching in Kansas City, Hamilton accidentally swallowed his chaw. He turned around and threw up all over the back of the pitching mound.

Tommy Henrich

Big Moments

Tommy Henrich was in awe of the Yankees when he joined them in 1937.

It's not as though Henrich didn't fit in—he played 11 seasons with the Yankees and produced some of the biggest plays in World Series history.

He produced the series-winning hit in 1947 against Brooklyn.

Two years later his home run gave Allie Reynolds a 1-0 win over Don Newcombe in the opener.

In 1941, it was Henrich who swung and missed a pitch that was misplayed by Brooklyn catcher Mickey Owens. "When I saw that little jackrabbit bouncing, I said, 'Let's go.'"

The Yankees went on to win that game and the series.

And The Difference Is . . .

" Catching a fly ball is a pleasure. But knowing what to do with it after you catch it is a business."

— Tommy Henrich

Miller Huggins

Do As I Say . . .

Miller Huggins not only managed some of the top players of all time, but he also had to sit on them as the Yankees were a raucous and partying bunch.

Shortstop Mark Koenig liked to tell the story about how Huggins would lecture his club on the ills of drinking too much, especially after losses.

Sometimes the players listened, most times they did not.

One early morning, at about 4 a.m., Huggins caught one of his pitchers breaking curfew. The hurler had a blonde on one arm and a red head on the other.

"Good morning, son," said the manager.

"Hi-yah, Hug!" replied the pitcher.

Later that same day, Huggins reamed his pitcher out for carousing and getting plastered in public. The manager threatened a fine the next time it happened, and the pitcher understood.

However, on the way out of Huggins' office, the player turned and asked who turned him in.

Reggie Jackson

Incredibly Edible

Reggie Jackson hit 156 home runs as a New York Yankee, 12 in postseason play. What's his recipe for success? Rice and greens.

"With greens and rice, I don't leave 'em (hits) on the warning track," Jackson once said.

"The Straw"

Reggie Jackson got off on the wrong foot when he arrived in New York in 1977.

Not only were players jealous of his five-year, $2.9 million deal, but he bucked ranks by declaring himself to *Sport* magazine that he was "the straw that stirs the drink."

That interview infuriated catcher Thurman Munson. Of the team captain, Jackson said, "Munson thinks he can be the straw that stirs the drink, but he can only stir it bad."

When Jackson told Munson some of the quotes were taken out of context, all Munson could say was, "For four pages?"

How About Some Onions?

"There isn't enough mustard to cover that hot dog," former Oakland A's teammate Darold Knowles said of Jackson.

Derek Jeter

A Dream Comes True

Playing ball for the New York Yankees is what Derek Jeter dreamed about while growing up nearby in New Jersey.

Once in a while his grandmother would treat him to bleacher tickets. While he admired the likes of Don Mattingly, Willie Randolph and Dave Winfield, he always pictured himself playing shortstop.

Reality arrived in 1996, a year in which the rookie would start at shortstop during the World Series.

"This is what you've always thought about," Jeter said at the dawn of a Fall Classic showdown with the Atlanta Braves.

"From the time you start playing ball, you think about playing in the World Series. And if you've ever

been inside Yankee Stadium, you think about playing here."

Star-crossed

When stars cross, sparks are bound to follow. Joe DiMaggio had Hollywood actress Marilyn Monroe. Derek Jeter had superstar singer Mariah Carey. Jeter dated the singer during the 1998 season but their romance broke up.

Hi, Derek (Insert Giggle Here)!

A quick bat, a solid glove and a strong arm can make you an All-Star, but youth and good looks will get you fan mail from adoring women.

Derek Jeter is a leader in the Yankee clubhouse for letters and remains the player most in demand among single women in New York.

"I've been here 42 years and I've never see girls go fanatical about a ballplayer like this," said Yankee Stadium vendor Kenneth Spinner.

Doubling Up

Winning the World Series and American League rookie of the year honor in the same year was a dream come true for 22-year-old Derek Jeter in 1996.

How long did he celebrate the championship? One month, and then it was back to work at Yankees camp in Tampa, Florida, fielding grounders and adding 15 pounds to his frame.

When teammate Mariano Duncan received a phone call from Jeter in Tampa, he wondered why his fellow infielder was in camp so early.

"What he's showing everybody," Duncan said, "is he wants to get better and better."

True, Jeter followed up his .314 first season with a .291 average as a sophomore. But by his third season, Jeter established a new home run record for Yankee shortstops with 19 in 1998.

Steve Kemp

Merge Ahead

One of the most severe fielding accidents in Yankee history was the result of two pieces of cotton.

In a game at Toronto's Exhibition Stadium, a pop fly was lifted into short right-center field. Second baseman Willie Randolph was running back on the ball while outfielders Jerry Mumphrey and Steve Kemp rushed in. Mumphrey called for the ball, only Randolph couldn't hear over the wind and Kemp couldn't hear because of the cotton balls he placed in his ears to ward off the frosty effect of the wind.

Randolph got the palm of his glove on the ball before Kemp slammed into him and then stepped on Mumphrey's foot. The ball fell loose, setting up a game-winning rally for the Blue Jays.

Mumphrey suffered a broken toe and Kemp severely banged up his shoulder.

What The Heck

S teve Kemp always hustled in whatever he did. Kemp once scored from first base on a two-out popout that was heading foul into the stands only to have the wind take the ball back in and deposit it on the line.

Just another day, he said.

"With two outs I had nothing else to do, so I figured I might as well."

Don Larsen

El Perfecto

Twenty-seven batters, 27 outs. A perfect game. It is a feat rarely accomplished by any pitcher and, until the afternoon of October 8, 1956, had not been performed on a stage as large as the World Series.

Larsen altered his pitching style as the season progressed, making it more difficult for batters to pick up what he was doing.

By ridding himself of a windup motion, batters had a tough time spotting the different grips he used for his pitches.

The National League champion Brooklyn Dodgers, which faced Larsen in Game Five that day, with the series knotted up at two games apiece, certainly hadn't faced Larsen much at all.

As the game moved into its later innings, Larsen tempted the baseball gods. Standing next to Mickey

Mantle, Larsen leaned over and said, "Wouldn't it be something if I pitched two more innings with a no-hitter?"

The Mick just walked away.

"We all got the same idea about that time and cleared away from Don," Mantle said. "Larsen wasn't nervous, but the rest of us were."

The last batter was pinch-hitter Dale Mitchell, a spray hitter. With a 1-2 count, Larsen got Mitchell looking as umpire Babe Pinelli rang him up on strikes.

Catcher Yogi Berra ran out to meet Larsen between home plate and the mound, leaping into his pitcher's arms.

Two Of A Kind

Don Larsen and David Wells are the only two New York Yankees to pitch perfect games.

Larsen performed his in the 1956 World Series against the Brooklyn Dodgers. Wells tossed his in May 1998 against the Minnesota Twins.

What is another link between the two? Both graduated from the same high school, Point Loma in San Diego.

Phil Linz

What'd He Say?

Clubhouses and team buses are loose places after a victory, but following losses sometimes it's best not to say a word.

In August 1964, the Yankees were swept in four games by the Chicago White Sox at Comiskey Park. While a team bus full of players, coaches and assigned media made its way to O'Hare International Airport, utility infielder Phil Linz broke out a harmonica he had just purchased.

Linz had no lessons on how to play and was trying to follow some scripted instructions on how to play the song "Mary Had a Little Lamb."

The off-key rendition irritated manager Yogi Berra, who was sitting in the front seat of the bus still stewing over the four losses.

The skipper had said something that Linz couldn't hear, so Mickey Mantle—never one to pass up a good joke opportunity—relayed to Linz that he should play louder.

Next thing anyone knew, Berra stormed to the back of the bus.

"Hey, Linz. Go stick that harmonica up your ass," Berra said.

Linz was stunned at first and then threw the harmonica at Berra, who promptly threw it back at Linz. However, Yogi's throw was off target and the harmonica hit first baseman Joe Pepitone in the knee. Playing it up, Pepitone pleaded for a medic.

Linz apologized to Berra the next day, but the manager still fined him $250.

After the story hit the news wires, executives from the Hoehner Harmonica Co. contacted Linz and offered him $5,000 to endorse their product.

As it turned out, the Yankees would be playing a winning tune a month later, winning the American League pennant by one game over the same Chicago White Sox.

Don Lock

Maybe They Won't Notice

Spring training cuts are the worst to handle. The notices come in the form of red tags or notes on a locker or a whisper from a messenger.

Clubhouse manager Pete Sheehy was the bearer of bad news for many Yankee hopefuls.

One year, minor league outfielder Don Lock tried his best to avoid being declared dead, a term players use for being cut. He crossed out his name atop his locker and then barricaded himself in the locker with sweatshirts, gloves and shoes.

Pretending his bat was a rifle, Lock would "fire" at anyone who approached his little foxhole.

In the end, Sheehy managed to get his message across.

Sparky Lyle

A Regular Laugh Riot

One of Sparky Lyle's favorite things to do was sitting on birthday cakes—while naked. He would be seen getting out of a coffin for laughs or give trainers and management a scare by showing up at spring training wearing fake casts.

Don't Try This At Home

Sparky Lyle posted a 13-5 record and 26 saves in helping the Yankees win the 1977 World Series championship.

Always the flake, Lyle took his championship ring and tried to cut the glass on his coffee table at home.

"Then I found out that the coffee table was worth more than my ring," he quipped.

S parky Lyle proved to be the Yankees' top relief specialist during the 1970s.

As effective as he was on the field, his off-field antics raised eyebrows. Lyle had a penchant for sitting naked on birthday cakes. He also had his teammates rolling in laughter after a life-after-death stunt one day.

Fred Stanley had a friend deliver a casket to the clubhouse, a way station before he converted it into a bar for his van. Lyle couldn't resist the opportunity to spring forth from the coffin, so he got dressed up in a hood-like surgical mask and painted the area around his eyes black.

Manager Bill Virdon liked to conduct pregame meetings and go over the opponent's strengths and weaknesses. Prior to the meeting, Lyle climbed into the casket and waited for the right moment to arise.

As Virdon went through a description of the Baltimore Orioles lineup, Lyle pushed open the top, sat up and said, "How dooooo yoooooou pitch to Brooks Ro-been-son?"

Virdon couldn't help but laugh, although he threatened to have Lyle remain in the coffin.

A pitcher's arm is his lifeblood, and Sparky Lyle wasn't going to have just any medical expert examine his wing.

Lyle's trainer with minor league club Winston-Salem (North Carolina) was a fellow named John Dennai. He was examining the arm of pitcher Kenny Wright one night and said, "Yep, looks like a case of tenderitis."

A perplexed Wright answered, "You mean tendinitis, don't you?" Dennai said, "Well, it's either tenderitis or tendinitis, one of those two."

Needless to say, Lyle refused to have Dennai check out his arm.

Sparky Lyle earned the American League Cy Young Award following a 1977 season during which he posted a 13-5 record and 2.17 earned run average over 72 appearances. His 26 saves certainly caught the attention of the Cy Young voters.

When a reporter asked Lyle what he was going to do with the award, Lyle told him he was going to build a lighted trophy case on his lawn and leave the plaque out there for 10 years.

"He wasn't sure whether to believe me or not," Lyle said later.

S parky Lyle made his major league debut with the Boston Red Sox.

In one of his early outings in Kansas City, Lyle was paired up with ex-Yankees catcher Elston Howard. Twice he shook off Howard's pitch call only to throw two balls and eventually walk the batter. Manager Dick Williams, as tough as they come, immediately gave Lyle the hook.

Afterwards, veteran Carl Yastrzemski questioned how a rookie could shake off a veteran catcher like that. Williams agreed and threatened to fine Lyle the next time he did that.

Howard then showed why he was such a pitcher's friend. He thought Williams' decision was wrong, and so he devised a system with Lyle whereby if the pitcher wanted to shake off a pitch call all he had to do was delay his windup for a bit more time. With the acknowledgment, Howard would then flash new signals.

S parky Lyle was rewarded with a contract extension and raise following his being named American League Cy Young Award winner in 1977.

However, that winter owner George Steinbrenner opened his checkbook for some incoming pitchers, some of whom commanded more salary than the veteran Lyle. The reliever was upset and held out at the start of 1978's spring training.

Following several frantic phone calls from Yankees' front office personnel, Lyle finally agreed to report some four days late. When Lyle and his wife arrived at the airport in Fort Lauderdale, Florida, Steinbrenner adviser Cedric Tallis greeted the Lyles, as did a 100-piece high school band which played "Pomp and Circumstance," the tune that usually greeted Lyle on his trips out of the Yankee Stadium bullpen.

Mickey Mantle

Worth Something

An autograph or a home run ball from Mickey Mantle was a prize to keep, even before he reached the major leagues.

Playing for the Joplin (Missouri) Miners, a Class C team in the Western Association, a powerful Mantle would often hit home runs that would clear the right field fence and sometimes carry into an orphanage.

One time, after he drove a home run through a window, the children hung out a sign saying: "THANKS FOR THE BALL, MICKEY!"

In fact, somewhere lies a trophy case signed by Mantle.

When the 1962 All-Star Game wrapped up, Mantle shared a taxi with American League All-Stars Rich Rollins and Camilo Pascual.

While the cab was stopped, a fan called out to Mantle asking to sign his trophy case. Mantle stepped out of the cab, crossed the street and did just that.

Wait, There's More

Fans who watched Mickey Mantle in his later playing days realized the rigors of everyday baseball life, a lack of proper training and well-publicized social outings took a toll on his body.

When Mantle was breaking into the pros, the first thing that caught scouts' attentions was his tremendous bat power. The second thing was his speed—soon enough the scribes were calling Mantle "The Commerce Comet," named after his hometown in Oklahoma. A New York sports writer timed Mantle from home plate to first base in 3.1 seconds, when no other athlete had been clocked in less than 3.4 seconds.

Bill Dickey told some writers, "You should time him on his way to second, when he's really moving. Nobody who ever lived can reach second base from the plate as quickly as Mickey Mantle."

With All His Might

M antle had one approach at the plate: swing the bat hard.

He never bought into the scholarly approach used by Boston Red Sox great Ted Williams. In fact, when the Splendid Splinter shared some of his tips with the Mick, Mantle's head would spin.

The mighty swing produced some prodigious blasts. On April 17, 1953, at Griffith Stadium in Washington, D.C., Mantle hit a ball off Senators pitcher Chuck Stobbs that carried out of the ballpark. It first cleared a 55-foot high wall behind the left field bleachers, bounced off a 60-foot sign and came to rest in the backyard of a nearby house.

A Yankees public relations man announced the shot as traveling 565 feet, although years later he admitted to have never left the ballpark to measure. The bat and ball were later sent to the National Baseball Hall of Fame at Cooperstown, New York.

⚾

For Your Information . . .

S ometimes it wasn't pure might which led to Mantle's success at the plate.

Bob Turley, who pitched for the Yankees from 1955-62, often studied the tendencies of opposing hurlers, and relayed useful information to Mantle.

Said Turley: "One day on the bench I was sitting next to Mantle and showed him that I could predict all the pitches. He said, 'God almighty, let's work something out.' So during all my years in New York, Mickey and I would have all kinds of signs based on my whistling to let him know what was coming."

Loosey-goosey?

M ickey Mantle had an uneven temperament, running from hot to cold on a daily basis. Of course, he had his loose side, and he wasn't afraid to show it to his teammates in a tight spot.

The Milwaukee Braves took a three-games-to-one lead in the 1958 World Series. Mantle showed up in the locker room wearing a trick arrow on his head, as if someone had shot him through the head.

He told his teammates they were in a tough bind and broke up the locker room with a cross-eyed face.

The Yankees came back to win that series in seven games.

No Fish Story

Mantle wasn't afraid to scam his teammates when a humorous opportunity arose.

One time he solicited dollars for a raffle of a ham, only there was no ham. Purloined of his pork prize, Jim Bouton got even during Mantle's fishing derby, winning the weight division title with a 10-pound fish he had bought in the store a day earlier.

Livin' (Not So) Large

The first professional contract Mickey Mantle signed in 1949 was for $400 to finish out a minor league season.

For his rookie season of 1951, the Yankees paid him $7,500.

The following year was the same, although he would receive a $2,500 bonus for staying on the roster until June.

Mickey and his wife, Merlyn, rented a small room at the Concourse Plaza Hotel. It had no stove, no refrigerator and no television set.

"We couldn't afford to rent a television set, at $10 a month," Merlyn said. "Mickey needed to send money home to help his family."

In retirement, Mantle made so much more.

With baseball card and collectible shows becoming ever so popular in the 1980s and 1990s, all ballplayers—retired and still active—started to command large appearance fees. A three-day show could net Mantle nearly $50,000.

Hey, Mister?

I n an interview with *USA Today*, Mantle told this joke: "You know, I dreamed I died, and when I got up to heaven St. Peter met me at the pearly gates and said I couldn't get in because I hadn't always been good. 'But before you go,' St. Peter said, 'God has six dozen baseballs He'd like you to sign.'"

Etched In Stone

T he dearly departed Mantle once told Yankee teammate Tony Kubek he wanted one thing written on his tombstone: "I was a good teammate."

Roger Maris

Ouch!

Roger Maris was not only a target of fans who disapproved of his chase of Babe Ruth's home run record, he also drew the ire of teammates on occasion.

Since Maris often liked to shut fans up with lines about how much money he was making ($70,000 a year), some of his teammates would encourage Maris to "hit them with your wallet."

Auspicious Beginning

It didn't take long for Roger Maris to become a Yankee legend.

His 1960 debut in pinstripes featured a single, double and two home runs.

He would finish the season with 39 home runs, one fewer than American League champion Mickey Mantle.

No Classic For Him

The World Series was not kind to Roger Maris. He batted .187 in 28 Fall Classic games from 1960-64—but he did provide several memorable moments:

• Maris homered in his first postseason at-bat.

• A year later his ninth-inning home run lifted the Yankees over the Cincinnati Reds in Game Three.

• In 1962, his fine defensive skills were displayed as he hustled to field a Willie Mays double and kept Matty Alou from scoring to secure a 1-0 triumph over the San Francisco Giants.

Pass The Mouthwash

Outlasting Mickey Mantle in the 1961 home run race and eclipsing Babe Ruth's immortal record of 60 by just one left a bitter taste with many Yankees fans who couldn't appreciate what Roger Maris had accomplished.

"People were reluctant to give me any credit," he said years later. "I thought hitting 61 home runs was something. But everyone shied off. Why, I don't know. Maybe I wasn't the chosen one, but I was the one who got the record. It would have been a helluva lot more fun if I never hit those home runs. All it brought me was headaches."

Called a "flop" by some writers after hitting 33 home runs the following season, Maris grew increasingly disenchanted as fans derided his home run production which dropped to 23, 26, eight and 13 the next four seasons. He was subsequently traded to the St. Louis Cardinals, a club he helped to win National League pennants in 1967 and 1968.

Forgiven

Maris stayed away from a number of Old-Timer's Games, but he did return to the 1978 affair at

Yankee Stadium. He was surprised when he received warm cheers.

"It's like obituaries. When you die, they give you good reviews," he said.

Welcome, Rog!

R oger Maris came from humble roots, so playing in New York was quite a shock for him.

"This city's too big," Maris was quoted as saying.

At least roommate Bob Cerv didn't believe him. "Don't ever let anybody tell you they don't like coming to a team like the Yankees," Cerv said. "The Yankees are over the tracks and up the hill."

At least Maris would have appreciated a nicer reception when he arrived in the winter of 1959 in a trade with Kansas City. Problem is, he was dealt for popular Yankee Hank Bauer.

"For the first few games I used to hear guys yelling for Bauer," Maris said, who silenced any naysayers with 39 home runs and 112 runs batted in during his 1960 season. A year later, he would break Babe Ruth's home run record with 61.

Billy Martin

The Glasses Come Off

Billy Martin was born Alfred Manuel (Billy) Pesano, but many people who crossed his path got to know him as Battling Billy.

One time Boston Red Sox rookie Jimmy Piersall tossed insults at Martin about his big nose, so Martin threw some rights and lefts at him under the grandstand at Fenway Park to settle the score.

Sometimes Martin used a little help. One day St. Louis Browns catcher Clint Courtney spiked shortstop Phil Rizzuto while sliding into second base. Martin started a brawl with Courtney, eventually knocking his glasses off. That's when Whitey Ford literally stepped in and smashed the glasses.

Yer Outta Here!

Martin was run out of plenty of ballgames by umpires, but perhaps none as bizarre as one night in Arlington, Texas.

A handful of calls had already gone against the Yankees and Martin had exercised his right to argue on several occasions.

Martin stewed in the dugout and shifted the cap on his head so the bill faced sideways. The umpire motioned for Martin to come out of the dugout and ordered the manager to fix his cap.

Martin refused and was promptly ejected, but not before kicking dirt on the shoes of the offended arbiter.

On Billy Martin:

" He's the kind of guy you'd like to kill if he's playing on the other team, but you'd like 10 of him on your side."

— Cleveland Indians general manager Frank Lane.

The Ol' Pine Tar Game

No one will ever accuse of Yankees manager Billy Martin of not taking advantage of any edge one of his players had or a verse in a rules book.

That approach brought about one of the strangest game circumstances of all time.

On July 24, 1983, the Yankees carried a 4-3 lead into the last inning of a game with the Kansas City Royals. That all changed when Brett deposited a two-out Goose Gossage offering into the right-field seats to give the Royals a 5-4 lead.

Martin went out to Tim McClelland and asked the home plate umpire to check the amount of pine tar on Brett's bat. Resting the bat across the 17-inch plate, McClelland noticed clearly the pine tar extended past the 18 inches allowable as set forth in the rules book. The home run would be disallowed.

So McClelland turned to the third base dugout, threw his thumb in the air to signal an out that ended the game. Brett was enraged, storming the field to confront McClelland. Brett had to be restrained by members of the Royals.

Meanwhile, the bat in question disappeared. Kansas City pitcher Gaylord Perry got a hold of it in the dugout and passed it to Steve Renko, who in turn handed it to Hal McRae. Eventually, the umpires had to retrieve the bat from the Royals clubhouse.

Third baseman Graig Nettles ribbed his buddy Gossage afterward.

"You came in and gave up a home and got a save?" Nettles asked.

"I'll take them any way I can get them," Goose replied.

The Yankees thought they had gotten away with a sneaky win. However, American League president Lee MacPhail overturned the decision, stating McClelland's ruling wasn't in line with "the spirit of the rule." He ordered the game to be picked up at a later date, with Brett's home run standing and the next batter up.

The Yankees resisted and almost didn't show up for the second finish, an affair which took 10 minutes on an off day set for August 18. The final four batters of the game—one for Kansas City and three for the Yankees—were retired.

"Mentally it really hurt us," Martin said. "We felt we had a game taken away from us because of a play that was illegal. It was hard for our guys to accept."

It was Mickey Mantle who introduced Billy Martin to the pleasures of hunting when they were Yankee teammates. Often they would go out hunting for ducks and other waterfowl.

On one offseason trip to Texas, Mantle played one of his legendary practical jokes on an unsuspecting Martin, only the plan backfired, so to speak.

Mantle had Martin stay in the car while he went into the house of a friend who was going to allow them to hunt deer on his property. While inside, Mantle's friend asked if Mickey would be willing to put down his ailing mule as a favor. Mantle agreed, but he didn't let on to Martin.

Mantle stormed out of the house and told Martin his friend wouldn't allow them to hunt on his property. "You got to be kidding," Martin said, shocked at the news following a five-hour drive. Mantle said, "No, I'm not, and I'm so mad that I'm going to go by the barn and shoot his mule."

Martin insisted Mantle not do it, but Mantle drove his car over to the barnyard, spotted the mule and let off a rifle shot into the sight-impaired critter.

Next thing Mantle knew, Martin let loose two rifle shots. "What the hell are you doing?" Mantle demanded. Martin had shot two of the farmer's cows, for which the ballplayers had to ante up some money.

Sometimes there are no cures to a losing streak. On several occasions during his managerial career, Billy Martin would throw the names of the nine players he wanted in the lineup into a hat and would have someone pull the names out to draw up the batting lineup.

B illy Martin brawled with opponents as much as he tangled with Yankee team members. However, his infamous Billy The Kid nickname was not conjured up from the famed gunslinger.

Casey Stengel was managing the 1948 Oakland Oaks of the Pacific Coast League. His club was made up of many veteran major leaguers who were let go or were longtime members of the P.C.L. Since Martin was the youngest member of the lineup known as the Nine Old Men, the nickname Billy The Kid seemed appropriate.

Don Mattingly

Donnie Baseball?

If Boston Celtics great Larry Bird is called "The Hick from French Lick," then fellow Hoosier resident Don Mattingly could accept being called naive upon his signing with the Yankees in 1979.

"Honestly, at one time I thought Babe Ruth was a cartoon character," said Mattingly, blaming his Indiana background on his failed baseball history lesson.

Um, Wrong Call

Early in the 1985 season, Don Mattingly told the media he thought a day off was more important than attending an optional workout during the midst of a tough stretch of games.

George Steinbrenner jumped all over Mattingly's comments.

"I'm disappointed in that young man's attitude," he said, citing the failure to show up as a lack of discipline.

Ten years later, Mattingly was roundly praised as the best Yankee player not to have played in a World Series. The left-handed hitting first baseman was not only named the 10th captain in team history but also finished a stellar 14-year career with a .307 average, 222 home runs and 1,099 runs batted in.

Work, Work, Work

Putting in time to work on his game was never a problem for Don Mattingly.

While attending Reitz Memorial High School in Evansville, Indiana, Mattingly used to take two hours of batting practice even before the team's regularly scheduled three-hour practices. It's no wonder Mattingly batted over .500 in both his junior and senior years, and led Reitz to an Indiana state title.

It was the same high school that a four-year-old Mattingly served as mascot.

Cap'n Don

D on Mattingly joined a distinguished list of Yankee captains in 1991. He led by example and by work ethic.

A mild-mannered Midwesterner, Mattingly knew when to pick his spots to address teammates.

In the midst of a minor hitting slump, Paul O'Neill had asked a coach if he would ever get another hit. Mattingly chimed in, "No, with that tired swing you may not."

A simple kick in the butt, from one perfectionist to another.

Movin' On Up

The year Don Mattingly claimed the American League batting title (1984), he wasn't even the starting first baseman at the outset.

Ken Griffey Sr. had that job. It didn't take long for manager Yogi Berra to make a switch, though.

Mattingly finished up edging teammate Dave Winfield for the batting crown (.343). He collected 207 hits, 110 runs batted in, 44 doubles and 23 home runs. He also led the AL in fielding with only five errors to his credit.

No Ring-a-ding-ding(s)

Don Mattingly batted .307 in 14 seasons as a New York Yankee. Unfortunately for him, he made the ballclub one year after a World Series appearance and left one year before its next, thus giving him the distinction—if you can call it that—of being the best Yankee ever to miss the Fall Classic.

Perhaps that is why Yankee fans—sensing the possible end to a great career—erupted when Mattingly saw his first playoff action in the 1995 American League Divisional Series with the Seattle Mariners.

The applause brought tears to the eyes of manager Buck Showalter, a former minor league teammate of Mattingly.

After hitting .417 in the five-game loss to the Mariners, Mattingly took the 1996 season off, barely keeping alive the notion of returning.

The Yankees beat the Atlanta Braves in the World Series, with Mattingly and his wife, Kim, watching from their home in Evansville, Indiana.

Then in January 1997, he called it quits for good.

"I am what I am, and I did what I did," Mattingly told a press gathering. "I don't feel cheated. I chose not to play."

His message to Yankee fans on Don Mattingly Day, on the last day of August 1997, matched his play.

"I tried to keep it pure," he said. "I tried to keep it simple, just play great baseball over the years. I hope you appreciated it."

The Buck Speaks Here

" People ask me all the time about whether Don Mattingly should be in the Hall of Fame," former Yankees manager Buck Showalter said. "Statistically, he might not match up, depending on what your criteria are. But he's a guy who supersedes any statistics when you evaluate him. Nobody in the history of baseball has more of a Hall-of-Fame character than Don Mattingly."

In The Blood

T he athletic genes in the Mattingly family were not left for just Don. His brother Randy—almost 10 years his senior—played quarterback in the Canadian Football League.

Don On Mike

M ichael Jordan gave up his basketball career to try his hand at baseball, but the Chicago Bulls star never left the minors.

Said Mattingly of the NBA scoring superstar: "I like to think, OK, Michael, you're number 23 all over the world, just not in this stadium."

Joe McCarthy

A Real Winner

There was only one way with longtime manager Joe McCarthy—winning.

Over 21 seasons McCarthy's Yankee teams compiled 1,460 wins and a winning percentage of .627, both franchise records. His Yankee clubs won eight American League pennants and seven World Series championships.

How important was baseball and winning to McCarthy?

One day a depressed McCarthy was greeted by his wife, who tried to cheer him.

"At least we still have each other," she said. To which he replied: "Yes, dear, I know. But in the ninth inning today I would've traded you in for a sacrifice fly."

"Einstein in Flannels"

It was said Joe McCarthy read nothing during the season unless it involved baseball.

"So I eat, drink and sleep baseball 24 hours a day. What's wrong with that?" he asked.

And he wanted his players thinking of nothing but baseball as well. To make his point, he had the card tables in the locker room smashed.

"This is a clubhouse, and not a club room," he said. "I want players here to think of baseball and nothing else."

Yankees general manager Ed Barrow said McCarthy's memory was one of the best he came across, a good thing considering McCarthy never took notes and never used charts. Pitcher Lefty Gomez tabbed McCarthy "Einstein in flannels."

Speaking of flannels, McCarthy actually had the team's caps and uniforms cut larger so his players would look bigger and stronger.

The Right Way

Joe McCarthy was a stickler for Yankee image long before George Steinbrenner happened along.

Jackets and ties were the order for road trips. So, too, were the team breakfast sessions set for 8:30 a.m.

In 1936, McCarthy drew up a famous list which became his Ten Commandments of Baseball.

1. Nobody ever became a ballplayer by walking after a ball.
2. You will never become a .300 hitter unless you take that bat off your shoulder.
3. An outfielder who throws back of the runner is locking the barn door after the horse is stolen.
4. Keep your head up, and you may not have to keep it down.
5. When you start to slide, S-L-I-D-E. He who changes his mind may have to change a good leg for a bad one.
6. Do not alibi on bad hops. Anybody can field a good one.
7. Always run them out. You can never tell.
8. Do not quit.
9. Do not find too much fault with the umpires. You cannot expect them to be as perfect as you are.
10. A pitcher who hasn't control hasn't anything.

Harumph!

Several sports writers took to calling Joe McCarthy the "push-button manager," once his team started winning, as if the players would win without their helmsman.

"I spend all my summers in Atlantic City and only come back for the World Series," McCarthy would grumble aloud.

The Point Is ...

Joe McCarthy picked a weird stage to prove a point. As manager of the American League All-Star Team in 1943, McCarthy did not use any of the six Yankees picked for the game to prove that he could beat the National League All-Stars without them.

He was right. The A.L. prevailed, 8-5.

Wilcy Moore

Getting Even (Sort Of)

A most improbable Yankee was an Oklahoman named Wilcy Moore.

General manager Ed Barrow had read an article in 1926 about a strong right-hander who had run up a 20-1 record in the Piedmont League. Despite protestations from a scouting staff that felt a 30-year-old hurler was too old, Barrow signed him sight unseen.

"Anyone who has a 20-1 record anywhere is worth taking a look at," Barrow said.

His instincts were correct. Wilcy went on to post a 19-7 record (6-6 as a starter) with 13 saves and a 2.28 earned run average in 1927. He went on to win a World Series game in both 1927 and 1928.

Moore went 29-15 from 1927-29 and, after two years away, went 7-6 in 1932-33.

As good as Moore was on the mound, he was awful at the plate. He batted .080 in 1927 (.102 in his career).

No doubt, he became a favorite of Babe Ruth, who used to tease Moore about his hitting. Ruth even bet Moore he wouldn't get more than three hits in a season. Moore won the bet, with six hits in 75 at-bats. He used the $300 to buy two mules for his farm, naming one Babe and the other Ruth.

Thurman Munson

(Not) Your Man For The Job

Manager Billy Martin named Thurman Munson captain of the New York Yankees in 1976, the team's first one since 1939 when Lou Gehrig retired.

While honored, Munson was also forthcoming about himself.

"I'll be a terrible captain," he said. "I'm too belligerent. I cuss and swear at people. I yell at umpires, and maybe I'm a little too tough at home. I don't sign autographs like I should and I haven't always been very good with the writers."

Kiss And Run (Home)

Thurman Munson was a three-sport star in high school.

To help stay in shape, Thurman would include seeing his girlfriend in his training plans.

"He was always playing some kind of sport," said Diane Munson, who knew Thurman since he was 10 years old and later married him.

"To stay in shape he would run the mile to my house, kiss me and run right back home."

.300? Absolutely!

There was no settling for mediocrity with young Thurman Munson.

Once told by manager, Ralph Houk, that he, a rookie, shouldn't be too concerned about hitting around .240 since .250 is all the club expected, Munson shot back: "Damnit. I can hit .300 in this league."

True to his word, Munson batted .302 and became the first catcher to win the American League Rookie of the Year award in 1970.

Move Over, Shamu?

S tanding 5-foot-11 and weighing 190 pounds, Thurman Munson resembled a football player more than a baseball man.

Busing to a spring training game in Florida one day, teammate Lou Piniella called out to the driver. "Hey, Bussy, let the walrus off at Sea World."

At least Piniella got a smile out of Munson.

"My build works against me," Munson said. "I'm a short, chunky guy. I'm not the athletic hero type. Fisk is tall, lean and more attractive."

Fisk was none other than Boston Red Sox backstop Carlton Fisk.

There was a fierce rivalry between the two throughout the 1970s as they were the top catchers the American League could offer.

"He got all the publicity and most of the All-Star votes," Munson recalled, "I don't hold it against him personally, but he's never been as good a catcher as I am. If we were on the same team, I might even like him, but he'd have to play another position."

Expert Foresight

F inancial security was foremost in Thurman Munson's mind as his career headed toward the end, but came earlier in a fatal plane crash.

Apparently, Munson was a sound businessman whose real estate and other ventures netted his family more $1 million.

Munson's financial dealings allowed him a few extravagances. That is why Munson learned to fly and bought a small jet plane. He figured the plane would afford him the chance to fly home to Ohio on occasion to spend time with his family.

However, Munson advanced to small jets too quickly, said his teammates.

On August 2, 1979, Munson was in the pilot's seat when the jet he was trying to land at Akron-Canton Airport crashed. Munson broke his neck and never got out of the plane, which went up in flames.

A Best Friend's Feat

Thurman Munson was one of Bobby Murcer's closest friends on the Yankees. Murcer had been reacquired from the Chicago Cubs only weeks before Munson's untimely death.

Murcer delivered a heartfelt eulogy at Munson's funeral in Ohio and, later that evening, honored his friend and team captain the best way he knew how.

The Yankees flew home from Ohio that very same afternoon. A somber crowd at Yankee Stadium watched the Baltimore Orioles jump out to a 4-0 lead. The Yankees drew closer as Murcer hit a three-run home run, his first Stadium home run in six years.

In the bottom of the ninth inning, Bucky Dent walked and Willie Randolph's sacrifice bunt attempt was botched by pitcher Tippy Martinez. Up stepped Murcer. Down 0-2 in the count, Murcer drove both runners in with a single to left.

The Yankee dugout emptied and mobbed Murcer at the bag.

"Everybody was so tired," Murcer said. "I think we were playing in the spirit of Thurman. I think that's what carried us through the game."

The clean-cut image that the Yankees adhered to for many years also allowed for simple protests.

Catcher Thurman Munson was upset with the way owner George Steinbrenner was handling Billy Martin's job status, so he grew a beard in protest. It turned out to be a huge furor in New York as the daily newspapers played it up with hair-raising appeal.

As a favor to Martin, Munson eventually shaved the beard in order to take the pressure off the embattled manager.

Graig Nettles

The Other Guys

A thletes like nothing better than being appreciated with a healthy round of applause from the fans.

It's the booing that drives them crazy.

Graig Nettles was able to reason away the derision he sometimes encountered while playing at Yankee Stadium.

"Since it's a two-team town, to keep my sanity I preferred to think that many of those who were booing me were Mets fans."

Exhibitions? Hah!

Nettles was never a fan of exhibition games. He openly derided the significance of the annual Mayor's Trophy contests between the Mets and Yankees. He also hated the exhibitions with the Yankees' upper-level farm teams.

"As a player you don't have your heart in them 100 percent because you know it doesn't count in the standings, and therefore, when you're not trying 100 percent, you don't go all out, and that's how you get hurt."

Sure enough, during an April 1983 exhibition at Nashville, second baseman Willie Randolph twisted a knee, designated hitter Don Baylor pulled a hamstring and pitcher Dale Murray damaged his toe.

Still, Nettles—who didn't play that evening—took a bit of satisfaction in watching Nashville rally for five runs to beat the Yankees.

"Those kids were as happy as if they had won the World Series," he said. "They were giving high-fives all over the field. . . . Most of those kids will never make it to the big leagues, but it'll be something they can look back to their whole life."

Testing: 1, 2, 3

Some umpires are confrontational, others like to make judgments on players. Graig Nettles and arbiter Ed Runge hit it off right from the start. Runge had developed a reputation for testing rookies, and fortunately Nettles knew this. In his second major league at-bat, Runge and Nettles shared talk about their San Diego backgrounds while the pitcher and catcher were out at the mound. Runge wished him well and promptly called a pitch that Joel Horlen had nearly bounced a strike. Nettles said nothing.

The next pitch was clearly a strike and Runge issued a ball.

"He gave me pitches like no other umpire," Nettles said, "because I didn't complain to him when he tested me. . . . Accept the calls, because in the long run you'll get the breaks."

He Got His Wish

Outspoken and moody, Graig Nettles was named the sixth captain of the New York Yankees in January 1982. This is the same third baseman who once said: "When I was a kid, I wanted to play baseball and join the circus. With the Yankees, I've been able to do both."

Outta Here

G raig Nettles had the peculiar nickname of Puff. Why? Said baseball broadcaster Joe Garagiola: "They call him Puff because he's always provoking fights and then when they start, puff, he's gone."

Gabe Paul

Bad Form

Gabe Paul was a baseball executive for many years when monies were tight and he was always looking for a way to save his team a little money, even when his decisions sent the wrong message.

The Kansas City Royals and New York Yankees split the first two games of the 1977 A.L. Championship Series, and the teams traveled back to Missouri. The Royals went on to win Game Three, leaving the Yankees on the brink of elimination.

When the Yankees got back to their hotel, traveling secretary Bill Kane—under the orders of Paul—instructed the players to pack their belongings and bring their bags to the hotel lobby the next morning for check out. This would expedite matters should the Yankees lose and head back to New York right away.

George Steinbrenner found out about the request and got heaping mad. There was no way he wanted his players to think that winning Games Four and Five was out of the question, so he had Kane rescind the original requests.

The Yankees won both games, 6-4 and 5-3, to advance to the World Series, where they beat the Los Angeles Dodgers.

Joe Pepitone

Hair Today, Gone Tomorrow

When Joe Pepitone started going bald, he would use two hairpieces, a large toupee for wear in the public and a smaller one when he had to wear his baseball cap. He also took to carrying a small hairdressing kit with him wherever he went to tend to his natural hair.

The small bag always had a hot comb, different greases, a hairdryer and glue for the hairpieces.

During one game, Fritz Peterson and Jim Bouton decided to play a little trick on Pepitone. Sneaking into the clubhouse, the pair filled Pepitone's hairdryer with talcum powder. After a particularly tough loss, Pepitone came out of the shower and turned on the dryer. Within seconds he was covered in powder.

Joe Pepitone

Loss or not, it broke up the entire clubhouse.

Burnin' It Up

Pepitone was giving a hot-foot (secretly sticking fired matches on someone's shoe) to one of his teammates one day not realizing that Phil Linz was doing the same to him.

One moment he was smirking in delight, the next he was hopping around the dugout trying to put his own flames out.

Incommunicado?

Pepitone never lived down a throwing error, which cost the Yankees a victory in the 1963 World Series.

A year later, back in the Fall Classic, Pepitone actually shook off a pick-off sign by pitcher Jim Bouton.

"He was standing there shaking his head, tiny shakes because he didn't want anybody to see," Bouton said. "It was the first time I ever saw anybody shake off a pick-off sign.

"Just for the hell of it, I gave him the sign again a few pitches later. I wanted to see if he'd shake me off again. He did."

Gaylord Perry

Billboard?

A lasting image of Gaylord Perry is the uniform he used to wear to some Old-Timer's Games.

It's unique in that the logos of every team he played for are emblazoned somewhere on the shirt. There are race cars with fewer emblems on board.

The Wet One

Since Perry has played with so many teams, there were few players who didn't learn of his spit-ball techniques, not that they found a way to hit the spitter either. "You know the situations when he's going to throw you a spitter," Yankee third baseman Graig Nettles said, "and you know it's coming, but it's still a very hard pitch to hit."

Greasy Kid's Stuff

Perry often placed Vaseline on areas of his uniform. Before he'd go into his windup he'd be touching his neck or his belt or his hat, planting the thought into the batter's head that he was "greasing up" even if he wasn't.

Another neat trick involved Perry's use of the rosin bag. He'd pick it up and flip it in his hand a few times before setting it down.

When he released the next pitch a puff of rosin would appear.

Fritz Peterson

Fast Cats

Jim Bouton and Fritz Peterson were perfect roommates for one another, even if Ralph Houk tried to
split them up one spring.

They used to race cars down the California coast-
line, playing loud Spanish music along the way. Their
trips to San Francisco always included a run past the
hippies in the public parks.

Bouton was telling Peterson one day about how
he thrived on nervous tension to pitch better.

So before Bouton's next start, Peterson came up to
Bouton and whispered in his ear: "If you want to see
your baby again you'll win today."

Lou Piniella

Set The Alarm, Grab The Bat

Hitting was a science for Lou Piniella.
He'd practice his swing whenever possible, even in the middle of the night.

Piniella gave up tossing and turning in bed one evening to work on a new batting stance. Using a bat he kept near his bed, Piniella was taking a couple practice swings when he was shocked by a scream. It was his wife, Anita, who had opened her eyes only to see a man standing over her swinging a bat.

"I could hardly blame her for the shriek," a sheepish Piniella said.

It was a rare day when Yankee teammates didn't spot Piniella practicing his swing in front of a mirror in the clubhouse.

Graig Nettles liked to poke fun at Piniella and his protege Roy Smalley.

"This is Leonard Nimoy along with Lou Piniella and Roy Smalley, 'In search of ... the Perfect Swing.'"

Smashing Porcelain (And Other Cracks)

B aseball players have often shown little or no regard for the amenities and equipment offered for their comfort, especially after a particularly bad outing.

For Lou Piniella, water coolers were usually the target of his outrage. Billy Martin had a penchant for smashing urinals.

At old Cleveland Stadium, there's a long walkway from the dugout to the visitor's clubhouse. After the Indians put up a six-spot in the first inning, Martin not only smashed out all the lights in the runway but also demolished another urinal.

Piniella was never one to pass up a good one-liner so he offered this. "I'm going to go out there tomorrow with a flashlight taped to my helmet so I can get back up to the clubhouse after the game."

Piniella let his temper get the best of him in the 1976 season. A home plate scrap with Boston Red Sox catcher Carlton Fisk resulted in bruised tendons and ligaments in Piniella's hand.

Weeks later, as the hand was just about healed up, a rough outing at the plate sent Piniella into a clubhouse rage. His misdirected attempt at smashing a stool against the wall found his hand slipping in between.

Nice 'N' Neat, You Hear?

George Steinbrenner was always a stickler for neatness. He dressed well and he wanted his players to look appropriate as well.

One spring training Lou Piniella showed up in camp with long hair. Clubhouse manager Pete Sheehy told Piniella he wasn't allowed to dress and was instructed to report to Steinbrenner's trailer office.

Piniella and Steinbrenner had the following conversation.

"Lou, you can't dress with hair that long."

"Why not? What has long hair to do with my ability to play?"

"It's a matter of discipline. I just won't have it."

The argument continued.

Said Piniella: "If our Lord, Jesus Christ, came back down with his long hair, you wouldn't let him play on this team."

Steinbrenner got out of his chair and had Piniella follow him across the street to a pool in the back of a motel. "If you can walk across the water in that pool," Steinbrenner said, "you don't have to get a haircut."

Point made. Piniella reported the next day with a nice and appropriate haircut.

Managing Just Fine

George Steinbrenner thought Lou Piniella would make a great manager someday so, in his usual course of taking action before thinking, he decided to make that point public.

Of course, Steinbrenner already had a manager in place—Billy Martin—but with that tumultuous relationship it was probably best to have an ace up your sleeve.

Piniella got his first crack at managing the Yankees on an interim basis in July 1985. Martin had to be hospitalized when a doctor accidentally punctured his lung while trying to administer a muscle relaxant shot for Martin's aching back.

Steinbrenner phoned Piniella in Texas, where the Yankees were just finishing up a series with the Rangers, and told Piniella he would be taking over the club for a few days. To Piniella's dismay, Steinbrenner neglected to call Martin first, so Billy had to hear the news from someone else.

The club flew to Ohio, and Piniella arrived at Cleveland Stadium early the next day to assume duties. He was informed by coach Doug Holmquist that Martin had called the clubhouse already and would have the lineup phoned in within an hour. The problems began when Piniella made his first mistake by failing to make out a lineup card—he thought coach Gene Michael did that since he always posted it for the players.

Martin kept in touch with Piniella via the telephone from his hospital bed in Arlington, Texas. With injured catcher Butch Wynegar serving as phone operator for a night, Martin called in each of the first three innings just to get updates and query Piniella on a few things. When the press caught wind of this after the game, their stories told of how Martin managed the Yankees from his hospital bed.

The Yankees won the first two games under the Piniella/Martin setup and then lost three. Prank phone callers tied up the phone line in the Yankees dugout, pretending to be Steinbrenner or Martin, infuriating the latter when his real calls couldn't get through. Players started questioning Piniella's moves. A fan yelled from the stands, " Is that your decision or is it coming from a hospital bed in Texas?"

By the end of the Indians series, Piniella was so flustered he took a souvenir baseball from his first win as manager and threw it into a urinal in the clubhouse.

"I had been made to look foolish on the field and in the dugout," Piniella fumed.

When he got home to New York, he told his wife he was quitting baseball altogether. However, calmer heads prevailed.

Steinbrenner and Martin both asked Piniella to return as hitting coach.

Willie Randolph

The Home Show

With Yankee Stadium playing host to its third All-Star Game in 1977, New York City product Willie Randolph made sure it was a special night in the Big Apple.

The starting second baseman collected a run-producing single. "I was a young kid in front of my home-town fans, my family," Randolph said. "I played the whole game. I was there playing with guys I had grown up idolizing—Rod Carew, Reggie Jackson."

Allie Reynolds

Historic Stuff

Allie Reynolds secured his place in history in 1951 as the first American League pitcher to hurl two no-hitters in the same season. On July 12, he won a 1-0 duel with former roommate Bob Feller of the Cleveland Indians, facing only 29 batters.

On September 28, the Yankees beat up on the Boston Red Sox, 8-0, only a funny thing happened on the way to his second no-no.

Ted Williams had wrapped up his 10th consecutive season of hitting over .300 and now stood in the way of Reynolds' glory.

Down 0-1 in the count, Williams fouled a fastball high behind home plate. Catcher Yogi Berra got under it, but failed to make the catch.

Reynolds helped Berra to his feet and said, "Don't worry Yogi, we'll get him next time."

Williams shot back at Berra. "You blew it. You son of a bitches put me in a hell of a spot. Now I've got to bear down even harder even though the game is decided and your man has a no-hitter going."

As far as Berra was concerned, the pitch almost worked once, it should again. Sure enough, a fastball was fouled off in the direction of the Yankee dugout and this time Berra made the grab to complete the no-hitter and the 1951 pennant clincher.

Mickey Rivers

And He Means It, Too

Mickey Rivers was the answer to the Yankees' base-running needs when he was acquired from the Texas Rangers in 1976.

Mick the Quick stole 93 bases over four seasons, 43 in his first season in pinstripes. However, to look at him, it seemed as though his legs were always pained as he took a slow walk to the home-plate circle.

Rivers was a carefree spirit who didn't let things bother him. Consider:

"Ain't no sense worrying about things you got control over, 'cause if you got control over them, ain't no sense in worrying. And there ain't no sense worrying about things you got no control over, 'cause if you got no control over them, ain't no sense worrying."

Happy Together

Marital disharmony cost Rivers dearly one afternoon. After spending a night away from home, Rivers was greeted at Yankee Stadium by his wife.

Several times, she plowed the Mercedes she was driving into the Cadillac he had taken to the ballpark. Then she slapped him around a few times in the parking lot before going home and burning all his clothes. He was forced to wear sweatsuits for more than a week.

Bet The Field

Mickey Rivers enjoyed going to the racetrack, even if his teammates were convinced he was the worst handicapper around.

"He would study those charts night and day," Lou Piniella said, "devour the *Racing Form* and pick nothing but losers. It got to be a joke."

Rivers would pick one way, and everyone with him would go the other way, Piniella said.

On one trip to Thistledown outside Cleveland, Rivers told Piniella that he had picked the winner of the sixth race and was banking $20 on the horse. Sure enough, Rivers' horse won and he cashed in. It was only later that Rivers admitted he had bet $20 on every horse in the race.

"Had to have a winner, Lou," he said. "Had to have it. Had to break my luck."

Phil Rizzuto

Taller Than He Appeared

Phil Rizzuto stood only 5 feet, 6 inches tall, but there was no better shortstop in his era.

Casey Stengel's "little fella" was the American League leader in double plays three times. Same goes for total chances.

Said starting pitcher Vic Raschi: "My best pitch is anything the batter grounds, lines or pops in the direction of Rizzuto."

Welcome, Stranger!

P hil Rizzuto was not welcomed to the Yankees with open arms.

Nixed by Casey Stengel in a tryout with the Brooklyn Dodgers, the Yankees liked what they saw in the Brooklynite and signed him to a minor league deal in 1937. Four seasons later he was up with the big club, only established veteran Frank Crosetti was patrolling the left side of the infield. Several veterans made it tough on Rizzuto to even get batting cage time until Joe DiMaggio came to the kid's rescue.

Step On A Crack ...

P hil Rizzuto was as superstitious as any player. He had to step out of bed on the same side every morning. He would never step on a baseline. He even had a great fear of insects.

Add One Stick Of Butter

Phil Rizzuto went right from the playing field to the broadcaster's booth upon retirement. He never stopped being a fan favorite, thanks to the charm he showed during his broadcasts.

He liked to keep things light when he could, sharing recipes over the air or running off a list of birthday wishes.

Holy !@#$

Phil Rizzuto was honored at Yankee Stadium on many occasions, but none as funny as a summer day in 1985.

The Chicago White Sox were visiting with none other than former New York Mets standout and future Hall of Famer Tom Seaver going for victory 300 (which he got in a gem of an outing). Rizzuto should have known the day wasn't quite his when the cow the club gave him—in honor of his broadcast call "Holy Cow"—stepped on his foot.

A Hall-mark

Admission to the Pro Baseball Hall of Fame was a long time coming for Rizzuto, who was finally voted in on February 25, 1994.

"I said, 'Holy Cow' and almost fell to the floor," he said. "I never gave up about the Hall of Fame as long as I was eligible and still breathing."

Charles "Red" Ruffing

We'll Show You

The Boston Red Sox obviously didn't learn their lesson when they traded 22-game loser Charles "Red" Ruffing to the Yankees following the 1929 season.

Not only could Ruffing hit (his 520 hits ranks him third best in history for a pitcher), he could pitch. In 15 seasons with the Yankees, Ruffing posted only one losing season. The right-hander played in seven World Series and posted a 7-2 record. He was voted into the Pro Baseball Hall of Fame in 1967.

Not bad for a man who lost four toes on his left foot in a mining accident years earlier.

Babe Ruth

Did You Know?

H ow did Babe Ruth get his nickname, Bambino? From the Italian neighborhoods. Babe is translated to "Bambino" in Italian.

After The Game

B abe Ruth's success on the field was only matched by his legendary lifestyle as a carouser and womanizer.

Writer Lee Allen described Ruth as "a large man in a camel's hair coat and camel's hair cap, standing in front of a hotel, his broad nostrils sniffing at the promise of the night."

When it wasn't time for baseball, it was time for having fun. Ruth was rarely seen in the hotels the club frequented, unless he was cavorting with the women of his choice.

Sometimes Ruth would go out looking for fun as soon as the team train pulled into town.

Outfielder Frank "Ping" Bodie was not only Ruth's roommate on the road but also his luggage carrier, it seems. All the players' bags were usually delivered to the hotel lobby, from where the players would pick up their belongings and bring them to their rooms. Since Ruth was rarely around for that drill, the dutiful Bodie would lug Ruth's bags to the room for him.

One day a reporter asked Bodie what Ruth was like when he and Bodie were alone.

"I don't know anything about him," Bodie said. The incredulous reporter rephrased the question, but to no satisfaction.

"I don't room with him," Bodie said. "I room with his suitcase."

Some Start

B abe Ruth played 2,120 games in the Yankee pin-stripes. While many were memorable, his debut in 1920 was not.

Manager Miller Huggins had Ruth play center field since "Ping" Bodie had left the team during spring training and Chick Fewster was hit in the head with a pitch and left speechless for weeks. Ruth dropped a fly ball in the eighth inning with two men on base and two outs, allowing the host Philadelphia A's to win.

The next day, a messenger interrupted play (something not uncommon in those days) and handed Ruth a package. Inside was a shabby brown derby purchased by Philadelphia third baseman Joe Dugan, the recipient of the "gift" play a day earlier.

Amidst the laughter of players and the crowd, Ruth smiled and donned the derby.

It would be another two weeks before Ruth finally hit his first home run as a Yankee. On May 1, Ruth belted a shot far over the roof at the Polo Grounds for his first of 659 regular-season homers in pinstripes.

Big Bat

B abe Ruth's first two years as a Yankee were two of his best. In 1920 he batted .376, hit 54 home runs (when 28 was his previous major league record) and drove in 137 runs. In 1921 he batted .378 with 59 homers and 171 RBIs.

It's clear Ruth had the upper hand in negotiating his next contract with Yankee management. An offer of $30,000 with bonus clauses was rejected. So too was a $40,000 offer. The Yankees finally proposed $50,000 for five years. It still wasn't enough.

"Make it $52,000," Ruth said. "There are 52 weeks in the year, and I've always wanted to make a grand a week."

In 1930, Ruth was only hours away from holding out—possibly for the season—after stalled contract talks. Finally, Ruth and co-owner Colonel Jacob Ruppert agreed to a two-year deal at $80,000 per.

It is said that when someone told Ruth that he was making $5,000 more than President Herbert Hoover, Ruth said, "Why not? I had a better year than he did."

Major Consumer

The story of Babe Ruth once eating a dozen hot dogs before a game is untrue, but the Bambino could really put the food away when he wanted to.

Frank "Ping" Bodie roomed with Ruth for two seasons. The 5-foot-8, 195-pound Bodie was championed as the team's biggest eater—that is, until Ruth came along.

"Anybody who eats three pounds of steak and a bottle of chili sauce for a starter has got me beat," Bodie said.

Act II

The diamond wasn't the only stage Babe Ruth performed upon. Starting in the fall of 1921, Ruth earned $3,000 per week on a 16-week vaudeville tour of the Northeast. Actually, the critics were fairly kind to Ruth, who demonstrated his baritone voice and his comic delivery.

Close Call

B abe Ruth had a penchant for fast cars. Speed limits and traffic signs meant little to Ruth, who had little difficulty talking his way out of traffic tickets due to his fame.

During his second season as a Yankee, a police officer—unconvinced or unimpressed with who Ruth was—arrested Ruth for speeding on Riverside Drive. Not only did Ruth pay the $100 fine, he was sentenced to a day in jail. Back then, "a day" ended at 4 p.m., so Ruth was happy he wouldn't have to miss all of that afternoon's 3:15 p.m. start.

Ruth had his uniform delivered to the jailhouse in lower Manhattan and put it on underneath his fine suit. Not heeding any advice from the judge, Ruth told someone in his jail cell, "I'm going to have to go like hell to get to the game. Keeping you late like this makes you into a speeder."

At four o'clock Ruth was released, and a crowd greeted him at the rear of the jail. This time, utilizing a police escort, Ruth made it to the ballpark in the upper half of Manhattan in 18 minutes and was inserted into the lineup.

A year earlier, in July 1920, Ruth was driving his four-door touring sedan from Washington, D.C., back to New York following a ballgame. Joining Ruth on the trip was his wife, Helen, outfielder Frank Gleich, backup catcher Fred Hofmann and coach Charley O'Leary.

While driving through Wawa, Pennsylvania, Ruth was driving too fast and failed to negotiate a curve. Ruth hit the brakes, but not soon enough to prevent the sedan from skidding off the road and flipping over. Charley O'Leary and Helen Ruth were the only passengers thrown from the vehicle, Ruth onto soft dirt and O'Leary onto the road's hard surface.

Babe thought he had killed O'Leary, who lay motionless. Ruth raised O'Leary's head and said, "Speak to me, Charley." O'Leary shook off his grogginess and demanded to know where his brand-new straw hat was.

All five passengers walked to a farmhouse where they stayed overnight. The next day they read a newspaper headline that trumpeted, "RUTH REPORTED KILLED IN CAR CRASH."

A Hub of Activity

Whenever a new pitcher served up a home run to Ruth, the Yankee would bellow in laughter about adding another to the growing list. It's not often any pitcher got the best of Ruth, save for one young left-hander named Hub Pruett.

Hurling for the St. Louis Browns, the 21-year-old Pruett struck out Ruth in their first meeting in May

1922. A month later, Pruett fanned Ruth again in a relief outing. Two days later, Pruett rang Ruth up three times in a starting role.

In a July matchup, Pruett induced a weak grounder back to the mound and fanned Ruth three more times. In August, a sore-armed Pruett answered the call in relief by striking out Ruth with the bases loaded.

A September meeting yielded a walk and another strikeout, the 10th in 14 plate appearances for Ruth. Finally, Ruth homered off Pruett in their 15th encounter. Ruth added three more strikeouts, a walk and a home run in the first five plate appearances against Pruett in 1923. Even though Pruett fanned Ruth only once more, he had retired the Babe on strikes 13 times in their first 21 face-to-face outings.

Pruett used his baseball earnings (he pitched for 10 seasons) to put himself through medical school. Dr. Pruett met up with Ruth many years later.

"I want to thank you for putting me through med school," Pruett said. "If it wasn't for you, no one would have heard of me." Ruth just smiled and said, "If I helped you get through medical school, I'm glad of it."

The Real Story Is ...

The story about Babe Ruth hitting a home run for a dying child was stretched somewhat.

In fact, an 11-year-old boy named Johnny Sylvester was hospitalized after being thrown off a horse.

A friend of the family had baseballs signed by the St. Louis Cardinals and New York Yankees and Ruth promised he would hit a home run during the World Series (he hit four).

After the Series, Ruth paid a hospital visit to the thrilled little boy.

Called Shot?

The most disputed legend of Babe Ruth is his called home run shot in the 1932 World Series. The Yankees won two games in the Bronx by scores of 12-6 and 5-2. There was considerable taunting between the two teams, a fact the Chicago sportswriters pointed out in their stories.

That only raised the fervor of Cubs fans when the series moved to Wrigley Field.

Charlie Root got the Game Three start for the Cubs but was rudely welcomed by the Yankees. Shortstop

Billy Jurges threw away the first grounder by Earle Combs, and Root walked Joe Sewell.

Ruth had already hit nine home runs during batting practice, and the fans greeted him with a chorus of boos. Having already pointed to the right-field bleachers before his at-bat, Ruth knocked a 2-0 fastball to that very spot. But there was more to come.

The Cubs rescued Root with some runs, tying the game at 4-4 in the fourth as Ruth misplayed a ball into a double. Most of the Cubs players were on the top of the dugout steps razzing Ruth as he stepped to the plate in the fifth. Root received a called strike. Ruth casually raised one finger. Following two balls, Root again got a called strike.

This time Ruth waved the Cubs players back into their dugout and raised two fingers. Root jawed with Ruth, who shouted back and gestured toward the hurler (which many people claim was Ruth pointing to centerfield). The next pitch was a change-up breaking down and away from Ruth, but the hitter reached down and deposited the ball deep into the seats in center for the longest home run in Wrigley history.

The Yankees won Game Three, 7-5, and Game Four, 13-6.

Actually, his first called home run in a World Series took place four years earlier, in 1928, against the St. Louis Cardinals. The Yankees had swept the first three games handily before the Cardinals put up a fight in Game Four.

Ruth homered in the fourth inning to tie the game at 1-1. Trailing 2-1 heading into the seventh, left-hander Willie Sherdel got two strikes on Ruth and tried quick-pitching Ruth while the hitter had his head turned while talking to catcher Earl Smith.

In the National League, quick pitches were allowed, but this was World Series play and it was agreed to beforehand by the league presidents that this would not be allowed. The Cardinals argued in vain while Ruth smiled from outside the batter's box. Ruth clapped when the argument ceased and exchanged words with Sherdel.

After two balls were issued, Ruth told Sherdel, "Put one right here and I'll knock it out of the park for you."

Sure enough, Sherdel did and Ruth deposited the ball into the right-field seats.

A Kind Gesture

The bat Babe Ruth used to hit his 50th home run in 1920 (he finished with 54) was auctioned off with proceeds going to help starving Armenians in Turkey.

Aware that people wanted a piece of history, Ruth trotted around the bases with the bat that produced his 56th home run in 1927.

A boy came out of the stands, patted Ruth on the back and grabbed the bat. Ruth carried the boy and the bat across home plate.

Don't Even Try It

S even hundred and fourteen home runs is an incredible figure, but it was wrong to try to cheat Ruth of a blast.

Tom Zachary served up home run number 60 to Ruth on September 30, 1927. Ruth poked a shot down the right-field line. Zachary argued the ball was foul to the umpire, but received no satisfaction.

Twenty years later, Zachary and Ruth met at Yankee Stadium. Ruth looked at him and said in a croaky voice, "You crooked-arm son of a bitch, are you still claiming that ball was foul?"

He Could Pitch, Too

B abe Ruth was a standout pitcher for the Boston Red Sox, but the Yankees frowned on using Ruth on the hill.

In 2,084 regular-season games with the Yankees, Ruth played first base 14 times and pitched on five occasions. He was 2-0 in 1920, 1-0 in 1921, 1930 and 1933.

For The Record

A common misnomer has the Baby Ruth candy bar named after the home run champ. In fact, the chocolate bar was named after President Grover Cleveland's daughter, Ruth, who was born in the White House.

A patent fight eventually did away with a chocolate bar that was named after him: Babe Ruth's Home Run Candy.

In fact, presidential protocol was lost on Ruth. On a very hot day at the ballpark in Washington, D.C., Ruth was heard to tell President Warren Harding, "Hot as hell, ain't it, Prez?"

Proving Them Wrong

Americans like to build up their heroes and just as quickly tear them down. Babe Ruth was to learn this during a troubled 1925 season.

During an exhibition tour following spring training, Ruth developed an intestinal abscess, the result of not taking care of himself, his doctor told him.

A 20-minute surgical procedure did the trick, but Ruth was never quite the same that season. He batted .290 and hit only 25 home runs in 98 games.

Writer Fred Lieb wrote Ruth off in an August piece.

"It is doubtful that Ruth again will be the superstar that he was from 1919 through 1924."

He went on to write how Ruth should be able to produce 30 home runs or so and a dependable .325 average for a couple years.

Ruth would average 50 home runs and hit over .350 in four of the next six seasons.

True Love

Babe Ruth christened the 1929 season by marrying his second wife, Claire, in a 6 a.m. ceremony on the day of the opener. The afternoon contest was eventually rained out, so Claire made her first Yankee Stadium appearance as Babe's wife the next day. Sure enough, Babe hit a home run and tipped his hat to her as he rounded third base.

Heartfelt

The Yankees held a Babe Ruth Day at Yankee Stadium on April 27, 1947, more than a year before his death. The following was his raspy speech:

"Thank you very much, ladies and gentlemen. You know how bad my voice sounds. Well it feels just as bad. You know, this baseball game of ours comes up from the youth. That means the boys. And after you're a boy and grow up to play ball, then you come to the boys you see representing clubs today in your national pastime. The only real game in the world, I think, is baseball.

"As a rule, people think that if you give boys a football or a baseball or something like that, they naturally become athletes right away. But you can't do that in baseball. You've got to start from way down, at the bottom, when the boys are six or seven years of age. You can't wait until they're 15 or 16. You've got to let it grow up with you, if you're the boy. And if you try hard enough, you're bound to come out on top, just as these boys here have come to the top now.

"There have been so many lovely things said about me today, that I'm glad to have had the opportunity to thank everybody. Thank you."

Pour One More

B abe Ruth succumbed to cancer, at age 53, on August 16, 1948. His body lay in state at the main entrance of Yankee Stadium for two days, during which time more than 100,000 people passed his coffin. His funeral was attended by more than 7,000 people.

Pallbearer Joe Dugan made light of the weighty hero's casket. "I'd give $100 for an ice cold beer," he said. Noted pallbearer Waite Hoyt, "So would the Babe."

A Little Extra Dough

B arnstorming tours were an avenue for baseball players to make some cash in the weeks following a
season.

Early in Ruth's career, he could command $1,500
for appearing in an exhibition contest. Following the
1920 season, Ruth joined a group of New York Giants
on a barnstorming tour of Cuba where he reportedly
made $40,000.

What's a player to do with all that money except
gamble it away? Ruth enjoyed going to the horse track
in Havana. He didn't particularly enjoy losing money,
though. On one race Ruth lost $25,000. By trip's end,
Babe's wife, Helen, had to buy the tickets for the boat
trip home.

Rollie Sheldon

Well, The Truth Is . . .

Growing old is the worst crime a baseball player can commit.

It's no wonder lanky pitcher Rollie Sheldon fibbed about his age when he broke in with the Yank-ees.

In 1961, Sheldon told the club he was 19 years old. He went on to post the best spring training of any rookie and won the James P. Dawson award as a result. However, before the team headed north it was discovered that Sheldon had actually served in the U.S. Air Force and attended some college.

His real age was 24.

The Yankees decided to keep the 6-foot-4 right-hander, and Sheldon rewarded them with an 11-5 record and 3.60 earned run average during his initial campaign.

George Steinbrenner

Sure-fire Bet

George Steinbrenner was an owner of the Florida Downs horse racing track, so it wasn't unusual for players to show up and plunk down a few bucks.

In 1978, Lou Piniella decided to plunk down some real money and invest in some racehorses during an auction at Hialeah near Miami.

Steinbrenner noticed Piniella and queried him as to what he was doing. Steinbrenner told him the horses at that particular auction were no good, so he led him to another private paddock where a sale was going on.

"This is where the good stuff is," Steinbrenner said.

Soon after the bidding began, Steinbrenner and Piniella agreed to go halves on a purchase. Piniella chose one filly, and received a nod of approval as the asking price soared to a final price of $43,000.

"We just stole one," a proud Steinbrenner confided. "We just stole one."

The filly's name was Proudly Dancing. Though the horse had never raced previously, Piniella shipped it to Monmouth Racetrack in New Jersey. A thunderstorm preceded Proudly Dancing's first race, but Piniella and the trainer decided to run her in the mud anyway.

Proudly Dancer started last and finished last. Subsequent starts were also unproductive. Eventually she was sold for $7,500.

Whoops!

There's something about telephones that drove manager Billy Martin crazy. He hated the idea that owner George Steinbrenner called him during games or in the middle of the night.

After one such call, Martin ripped the phone right out of the wall in the clubhouse. When Steinbrenner queried a trainer as to why Martin's phone was out of order, he was informed why it happened. The Boss' reply: "Okay, tell him I'll call him tomorrow."

Another time Steinbrenner called the dugout and instructed Martin to fine catcher Thurman Munson for not wearing his baseball cap. One night at Chicago's Comiskey Park, third baseman Graig Nettles fielded a call from an irate Steinbrenner. Martin played it up as though an impersonator made the call and hung up, stunning Nettles. "Maybe he'll learn not to call down here anymore," Martin said.

S hortstop Gene Michael had a cold trick pulled on him one day in Texas.

A teammate shoved half of a hot dog into a finger hole on Michael's glove.

When the infielder ran out to his position and tried inserting his hand he was shocked at the discovery of something foreign, jumped up and threw his glove high in the air.

Compounding the joke was owner George Steinbrenner's reaction. He had a batboy fetch the wiener out of the glove and bring it to him. He was going to fine whoever put the hot dog wiener in the mitt in an incident which became known as The Great Wiener Caper.

Casey Stengel

The First Shot

It is often thought that Babe Ruth must have been the first player to hit a home run at Yankee Stadium in a World Series game.

In fact, it was Casey Stengel of the New York Giants who did it in 1923. In fact, Stengel homered in two games at Yankee Stadium, both Giants victories. While running the bases following the second homer, Stengel thumbed his nose at the Yankee bench.

Yankees owner Colonel Jacob Ruppert filed a complaint with baseball commissioner Kennesaw "Mountain" Landis, who denied the request for punishment. Babe Ruth was asked how he felt about Stengel getting away with his impish stunt.

"I don't mind," he said. "Casey's a lot of fun."

It's Crazy Over There

During his early playing days, Casey Stengel played for a minor league team in Maysville, Kentucky. Fittingly, an insane asylum was located just beyond the outfield fence.

The residents used to whoop and holler whenever Stengel left the field because he would practice his slide into third base before heading into the dugout.

How birdy was Stengel? In 1918, as a member of the Pittsburgh Pirates, the fans at Ebbets Field welcomed the former Brooklyn Dodger with a chorus of boos. With that, Stengel removed his baseball cap and a little sparrow flew out.

"The Old Perfesser"

The most famous nickname attached to Charles Dillon "Casey" Stengel was "the old Perfesser." He did not receive that moniker as field manager of the Yankees or Mets, two clubs he managed while he was in his 70s. In fact, he picked up that nickname in 1914, when he was 24 years old, during a spring training coaching stint with the University of Mississippi.

Say It Again, Casey

During one spring training in Arizona, Mickey Mantle was clubbing the ball as he never had before.

Naysayers said the thin desert air was the reason for it. Not so, Casey said, in his own form of "Stengelese."

"All I hear from you guys is talk about the stratmosphere," Stengel said, obviously referring to the atmosphere. "All I can say is the rest of these guys are hitting in the same air as this kid, and they ain't knockin' balls over the fences the way he is. Stratmosphere my eye! Mantle just hits hard, and you'll see that when we play in other places."

Second Show At 11

Casey Stengel was a master of one-liners.

"Anyone comes looking for me, tell 'em I'm being embalmed," he would say. Not long after being named the 1949 manager of the year, Stengel ran into the previous year's selection, Billy Meyer of the Pittsburgh Pirates.

"Ain't it funny, Bill, how all of a sudden I got so smart and you got so dumb?"

Tall Task

W hat kind of pressure was Casey Stengel dealing with as manager of the Yankees?

"The Yankees don't pay me to win every day—just two out of three."

Over 12 seasons, Stengel's Yankee teams won 1,149 games and won every American League pennant between 1949 and 1960, with the exception of 1954 and 1959. His teams also won seven World Series titles.

Accurate

G reg Goosen said the best thing Stengel ever said about him was the following.

"We got a kid here named Goosen, 20 years old, and in 10 years he's got a chance to be 30."

Really, He Said These

Some more Stengelese quotables:
- "Satchel Paige threw the ball as far from the bat and as close to the plate as possible."
- To Tommy Henrich: "I don't want you to sit in a draft. Don't slip and fall in the shower. And under no circumstances are you to eat fish, because them bones can be murder. Drive carefully, and stay in the slow lane, and sit quietly in the clubhouse until the game begins. I can't let anything happen to you."
- "They say some of my stars drink whiskey, but I have found that the ones who drink milkshakes don't win many games."
- "Right now we playin' bad every place. Not hittin', not pitchin' and not fieldin' too good. And judging by what I read in the newspapers, the Yankee writers are in a slump, too."
- "Left-handers have more enthusiasm for life. They sleep on the wrong side of the bed and their heads get more stagnant on that side."
- "If we had batting helmets when I was playing, John McGraw would have insisted that we go up to the plate and get hit on the head."
- "As great as the other men were on the ballclub, there comes a time when you get a weakness and it might be physical."

Joe Torre

Heartfelt

Rocco Torre died of a heart condition while watching television as his brother, Joe, managed the Yankees.

At the wake, Joe took the lineup card from that game and placed it in his brother's coffin along with a Yankee cap.

Frank Torre, a member of the 1957 and 1958 Milwaukee Braves World Series teams, was the next family member to have heart problems. While Joe was leading the Yankees to a pennant, Frank waited for a heart transplant. Frank got his new heart in the midst of the playoffs.

Finally, A Ring!

J oe Torre played 18 years and managed for 14 more with no World Series ring.

It wasn't until the Yankees finished off the Atlanta Braves in Game Six of the 1996 Fall Classic that his streak of 4,272 games without the ring would come to an end.

"I've never been so happy," Torre said after taking a celebratory victory lap around Yankee Stadium. "I never thought this would happen to me."

His players thought it would.

"He kept saying, 'We will win this thing,'" reliever John Wetteland said. "Joe was the constant. No matter what happened, he never got too high or too low. He remained a rock for this team."

David Wells

The Ink Spots

How important is family to David Wells? He has a tattoo of his late mother, Eugenia Ann, on his chest and another tattoo of his son, Brandon, on his shoulder.

Chat Me Up

Time-honored tradition says leave the pitcher alone while a no-hitter is in progress. David Wells knows that, but he craved attention during his perfect game bid against the Twins.

Not one player bit for fear of tempting fate.

"I just wanted to talk so it would ease my mind a little bit," Wells said, "but no one would come near me."

Finally, fellow starting pitcher David Cone decided to break the tension by suggesting that Wells break out his knuckleball. While Wells appreciated the chat, he did not take Cone's advice. Reaching the dugout after the eighth inning, Cone told him, "You showed me nothing out there, you wimp."

In the final inning, Wells got Jon Shave to pop out, struck out Javier Valentin and then got Pat Meares to pop out to rightfielder Paul O'Neill.

"This is great!," Wells shouted as he was congratulated by catcher Jorge Posada and the rest of his jubilant team.

A Real Gem Of A Guy

To show his appreciation to his teammates for making a perfect game possible, David Wells purchased gold diamond rings for each of them. Each ring had "Perfect Game" engraved on the top with the linescore and date on the sides.

Mad Hatter

D avid Wells is a historian of baseball, particularly of home run legend Babe Ruth, with whom he shares certain portly physical attributes. Wells is such a fan of the Bambino that he actually purchased a hat worn by Ruth and wanted to use it as his own. He was dissuaded from doing so by the team.

Dave Winfield

Bird-dropping

Every player gets fined in baseball's kangaroo courts—sessions when everybody is liable for miniscule fines for missing signs and making mistakes, on and off the field—but how many players get fined by local magistrates for something that happened on the field?

Ask Dave Winfield.

The Yankee outfielder was warming up his arm between innings at Exhibition Stadium in Toronto, when the ball he threw in the direction of a seagull actually hit the bird in the throat and killed it. It took several pitches in the ensuing inning before anyone figured out the bird was deceased.

Following the game, two plainsclothes officers arrested Winfield and took him to the police station. The

Yankees' team plane was delayed a half hour waiting for Winfield to post $500 bond on a cruelty to animals charge.

While annoyed at the delay, Winfield's teammates were quick to make light of the event.

"Hey, Dave, did you plead not "gull-ty?'" asked Graig Nettles.

Manager Billy Martin pondered the moment and sarcastically told some sports writers: "Maybe when the Blue Jays come to New York next week, we should hold a memorial service for the bird. We can bury it back there by the monuments with the Babe."

The ribbing went on for weeks. Fans at opposing ballparks flapped their arms like wings whenever Winfield came to the plate.

They All Wanted Him

Dave Winfield possessed great athletic skills. It is no wonder that he was drafted by four professional teams in the American Basketball Association, National Basketball Association, National Football League and Major League Baseball.

Um, Nevermind

The World Series stage is what Dave Winfield wanted the most in his career.

It turned out to be his undoing.

During the 1981 Fall Classic with the Los Angeles Dodgers, Winfield managed just one hit in 22 at-bats.

The rest of his Yankee days were marked with doom as owner George Steinbrenner tabbed Winfield "Mr. May," an obvious contrast to Reggie Jackson's heroics as "Mr. October."

Butch Wynegar

What Was That?

There's always a danger in having pitches called from the dugout.

The Yankees were mired in a seven-game losing streak late in the 1985 season when they locked horns with the Baltimore Orioles.

The game was tied at 2 in the seventh inning. Baltimore's Alan Wiggins was on first base and Rich Bordi was pitching to Lee Lacy. With a 2-0 count, catcher Butch Wynegar looked into the dugout for a sign and saw manager Billy Martin call for a pitchout. Bordi threw wide, but Wiggins never strayed off the bag. He walked Lacy on the next pitch and Cal Ripken Jr. knocked in the winning run.

Wynegar would learn later that Martin did, in fact, scratch his nose because it itched; he never called for a pitchout.

Yankee Miscellaneous

What A Playoff!

The three-ring circus that was George Steinbrenner, Billy Martin and Reggie Jackson kept the Yankees on the back pages of the New York tabloids during the summer of 1978 but not at the top of the American League East standings.

The Boston Red Sox held a comfortable lead, and tensions were getting hot in the Yankee clubhouse. Jackson had been suspended by Martin for five games for failing to follow signals. Martin felt he wasn't being backed up by Steinbrenner, and eventually snapped, throwing out the famous line, "One's a born liar and the other is convicted."

Martin's farewell came before television cameras in a Kansas City hotel on July 25.

In stepped mild-mannered Bob Lemon to take over the job. Two weeks into the job, on August 19, the Yankees still trailed the Red Sox by nine games. A solid run reduced the gap to four just as the Yankees visited Beantown for a four-game series. The Yankees ripped through the Red Sox, scoring 42 runs on 67 hits. New York moved into a tie for first place, having erased a 14-game deficit in just 53 games.

Inside a week, the Yankees had taken a 3 1/2 game lead but the Red Sox wouldn't quit. Boston closed the season with seven consecutive wins, the last a 5-0 shutout of Toronto. Meanwhile, Catfish Hunter failed to nail down the clincher against Cleveland as the Indians prevailed, 9-2.

Both teams finished at 99-63. The season would be extended by one more game, a playoff to be played at Boston's Fenway Park.

"If we lose we can blame it on George (Steinbrenner) since he lost the coin toss," third baseman Graig Nettles said of the playoff site determination.

A splendid fall afternoon greeted two teams who were as loose as they come, odd considering what was at stake. Yankees starter Ron Guidry (already 24-3 at that point) served up a second-inning home run to Carl Yastrzemski and a sixth-inning RBI single to Jim Rice. Meanwhile, Mike Torrez carried a shutout into the seventh inning.

Chris Chambliss and Roy White reached on singles, but Jim Spencer flew out for the second out of the inning. Up stepped light-hitting shortstop Bucky Dent, who had just four home runs and was hitting an anemic .140 over the previous 20 games. Dent stood in and promptly fouled the second pitch off his foot.

As trainer Gene Monahan tended to Dent, Mickey Rivers handed Dent another bat. "Here, use this. I feel it will be lucky for you," Rivers said.

He wasn't kidding. Torrez hung a slider and Dent lofted a fly ball to left field that just wouldn't come down as it lazily carried over the famed Green Monster in left field for a three-run home run. "Bucky Dent had turned Fenway Park into the world's largest morgue," said Lou Piniella.

Thurman Munson kept the rally alive with a RBI double to knock in Rivers, who had walked and stolen second. Reggie Jackson homered an inning later to give New York a 5-2 lead heading into the bottom half of the eighth.

Jerry Remy doubled off closer Goose Gossage, and Yastrzemski singled him home. Carlton Fisk singled and Fred Lynn followed suit, cutting the lead to one. Gossage got out of the rally by fanning slugger George Scott.

A blinding sun gave Piniella fits in right field. With three outs to go, Dwight Evans popped out and Rick Burleson walked. Up stepped Remy, who hit a sinking liner to right. Piniella lost sight of the ball, but ran to where he thought it was going. Sure enough, he saw it just in time to lunge and corral the bouncing ball. He threw a lined shot to third baseman Nettles, holding Burleson, representing the tying run, at second base.

"Was that me or God who threw that ball?" Piniella pondered later.

Piniella made a catch on Jim Rice's fly ball to right-center but could not prevent Burleson from moving up to third base on the sacrifice. Up stepped Boston hero Carl Yastrzemski.

Nettles had seen Yaz power the Red Sox to the 1967 A.L. pennant over his own Minnesota Twins, and he prayed it wouldn't happen again.

"How about a pop-up right now?" Nettles said to himself, before changing his tune. "Not to me. Please, not to me."

Meanwhile, Gossage had no question as to what he was going to throw. "I wasn't going to mess around with any breaking junk," he said. "I wasn't going to get beaten by anything but my best. Yastrzemski's the greatest player I ever played against. I just wound up and threw it as hard as I could. I couldn't tell you where."

Yaz swung at Gossage's first delivery, a high fastball, and fouled it off in the direction of Nettles, who made the catch to wrap up the division title.

Piniella was grateful to God for having the opportunity to be on the field that day.

"I was excited for the moment, for myself, my family and my teammates. Most of all, I was excited for the organization. We understood the Yankee tradition that day. Even if none of us was a Ruth or a Gehrig or a DiMaggio or a Mantle, we had each carved our own niche in Yankee history, and that was something to be very proud of."

The Yankees not only beat the Kansas City Royals for the third year in a row in the A.L. Championship

Series, but also beat the Los Angeles Dodgers in the World Series for the second consecutive season.

Yankee Stadium

The House

Yankee Stadium was built in less than nine months at a cost of $2.5 million.

Ground was broken on May 5, 1922, as the Yankees played their 10th and final season at the Polo Grounds in upper Manhattan.

Not only did "The Yankee Stadium" (as it was originally known) have the largest capacity of any park of its time, it was the first to use the word "stadium."

The new ballpark opened on April 18, 1923, with a crowd of approximately 60,000 people braving the chilly weather (although the original announced crowd was 74,217, far beyond capacity).

New York Governor Al Smith threw out the first pitch and Babe Ruth was presented with a bat in a glass case.

The home plate umpire was none other than Tommy Connolly, who had called the first New York Highlanders game in 1903.

It was only fitting that Ruth hit the first home run in Yankee Stadium history, a third-inning three-run poke into the right-field bleacher seats off Howard Ehmke.

Before the game, Ruth had said, "I cried when they took me out of the Polo Grounds. Boy, how I used to sock 'em in there. I'd give a year of my life if I can hit a home run in the first game in this new park."

Way Out There, And Still In Here

The first season at Yankee Stadium saw 20 inside-the-park home runs, an astounding figure unless one considers the field's dimensions.

While the lines were short (296 feet in right, 301 in left), center field was nicknamed "Death Valley" for its 461-foot depth.

Dandy Location

T he site for Yankee Stadium, at the mouth of Crowell's Creek, was selected by owner Colonel Jacob Ruppert.

Having been kicked out of the Polo Grounds by the New York Giants tenants, Ruppert wanted to build a facility within sight of the Polo Grounds. It just so happened to be the same place baseball was born in the Bronx with the 1866 advent of The Unions of Morrisania team.

They Can See Clearly Now

T he remodeled Yankee Stadium opened to over 52,000 fans on April 15, 1976.

Although there were more than 11,000 fewer seats, all the seats in the new ballpark were unobstructed.

Brand-spanking new, the ballpark wasn't received glowingly by veterans.

"They changed a lot of it," Fred Stanley said. "There were some things about it that were the same, but it wasn't the old Yankee Stadium."

Radio Days (And Nights)

America grew up listening to World Series games on the radio, including games being played at Yankee Stadium.

As a result, the facility became a destination point for world travelers.

"When I was a kid," said right-handed reliever Pedro Ramos, "I used to listen in Cuba on the radio to the World Series and hear names like Yogi Berra and Joe DiMaggio. I got them in my head. I knew that Yankee Stadium was history and like somebody wants to see the Grand Canyon or one of the wonders of the world, to me Yankee Stadium was and is the wonder of the baseball world."

Adds infielder Phil Linz: "It is the most magic baseball park ever built. Playing there as a Yankee was like being in the Marines, the feeling that you were in a special ballpark, special town, special uniform, special history."

"Just walking into Yankee Stadium chills run through you," said pitcher Jim "Catfish" Hunter.

Don Zimmer

Just "Zim"

Don Zimmer has been around the game of baseball for what seems like forever.

He's managed against the Yankees, for the Yankees (on an interim basis) and has served as the right-hand man for Yankee managers. His knowledge of the game is immense, matched only by his affability and humor.

One time while the Yankees were struggling and Zimmer was coaching third base, he had a couple runners thrown out at home plate. He walked back into the dugout and proclaimed, "Aw, hell, I'm just trying to take some of the pressure off Roy (Smalley)." Smalley was struggling at the plate.

Using His Head

Zimmer was hit in the head with a fastball while playing for the Dodgers, and doctors had to put a metal plate in his skull.

One day the radio in Graig Nettles' locker was drawing a lot of interference.

"It must be you, Zim," Nettles said. "The plate in your head is messing up my radio!"

BIBLIOGRAPHY

Berger, Phil. (1998). *Mickey Mantle: Biography.* Random House Value Publishing, Inc.

Berra, Lawrence Peter, & Horton, Thomas N. (1989). *Yogi: It Ain't Over.* McGraw-Hill Publishing Company.

Bouton, Jim. (1970). *Ball Four: My Life and Hard Times Throwing The Knuckleball in the Big Leagues.* The World Publishing Company.

Creamer, Robert W. (1974). *Babe: The Legend Comes to Life.* Simon and Schuster.

Frommer, Harvey. (1997). *The New York Yankee Encyclopedia.* Simon & Schuster Macmillan Company.

Gallico, Paul. (1942). *Lou Gehrig: Pride of the Yankees.* Grosset & Dunlap.

Nettles, Graig, & Golenbock, Peter. (1984). *Balls* G.P. Putnam's Sons.

Piniella, Lou, & Allen, Maury. (1986). *Sweet Lou.* Bantam Books.

Winfield, Dave with Parker, Tom. (1988). *Winfield: A Player's Life.* W.W. Norton & Company.

Ken McMillan is an accomplished sportswriter and columnist in the Hudson Valley of New York State. He has been honored by The Associated Press and Gannett News Service for his work, notably for a project commemorating the 50th anniversary of Jackie Robinson breaking the color barrier in baseball. He has covered the Yankees, Mets and minor league Hudson Valley Renegades. He also worked two years as media relations director and assistant general manager of the Spartanburg (S.C.) Phillies of the South Atlantic League. He is 34 years old, and this is his first book.

Bob Jackson is a lifelong resident of Marion, Illinois. He is a retired art teacher and coach. Bob is a graduate of Southern Illinois University, Carbondale. He has been an avid baseball fan since the early 1940s.

Other *Daily News* Titles

Yogi Berra: An American Original

An American Original represents the most complete collection of Yogi Berra materials ever published. With over 150 classic photographs, Yogi's Hall of Fame career is captured in beautiful detail—including rarely seen pictures from his early years in Yankee pinstripes, to his World Series heroics on the great Yankee teams of the 1950s and early 1960s, and concluding with his life after baseball.

1998 • 218 pp • 8 1/2 x 11 hardcover • ISBN 1-57167-250-8 • $29.95

Yankees '98: Best Ever

This full-color retrospective commemorates the entire Yankees season from the pre-season arrival of El Duque, to David Wells' perfect game, to the Yankees' unprecedented achievements throughout the post season. This book includes week-by-week review of the season, complete post season box scores, player profiles and much more.

1998 • 156 pp • 8 1/2 x 11 paperback • ISBN 1-58261-030-4 • $19.95

Joe DiMaggio: An American Icon

From the very beginning to today's headlines, the *Daily News* has been there covering the life and career of Joe DiMaggio. In a positive and upbeat point of view this book will cover Joe's entire career plus the public aspects of his relationships with Marilyn Monroe, his family and his life after baseball.

1999 • 192 pp • 8 1/2 x 11 hardcover • ISBN 1-58261-037-1 • $29.95

Big Town Big Time

by Jay Maeder, editor Daily News

Big Town Big Time is the colorful panoply of politics, culture, crime, sports, etc....The personalities, the events, the flow of time. Including *The Luckiest Man on the Face of the Earth-Lou Gehrig Day 1939*, and *And Sometimes Connect-The Babe Comes Back, 1923*.

1998 • 198 pp • 9 1/2 x 13 hardcover • ISBN 1-58261-028-2 • $39.95

Jets: Broadway's 30-Year Guarantee

Broadway's 30-Year Guarantee takes fans back relive the Jets' 1968 season and their astonishing Namath-guaranteed 16-7 triumph in the 1969 Super Bowl. Each game of that season of destiny is recounted. There are the player profiles, in-depth coverage of Super Bowl III and more than one hundred classic photos, drawn from the archives of the *New York Daily News*, that combine to make this book a complete retelling of New York's most memorable day in sports. Foreword by Hall of Famer Don Maynard.

1998 • 192 pp • 8 1/2 x 11 hardcover • ISBN 1-58261-016-9 • $29.95

Jets: Broadway's 30-Year Guarantee (Leatherbound Edition) $99.95

Limited edition of 500
Signed by:
Don Maynard, Larry Grantham, Matt Snell, Gerry Philbin and George Sauer

Available at your local bookstore or by calling
1-877-424-BOOK